P9-DFY-692

For These Fragile Times

Joyce Landorf

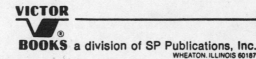

VICTOR

BOOKS a division of SP Publications, Inc.
WHEATON, ILLINOIS 60187

Offices also in
Whitby, Ontario, Canada
Amersham-on-the-Hill, Bucks, England

Mrs. Landorf's selections in this book are favorites from her column, "I've Been Thinking," which she wrote over a period of years for *Power for Living*.

Recommended Dewey Decimal Classification: 248.3
Suggested Subject Heading: MEDITATIONS

Library of Congress Catalog Card Number: 84-50138
ISBN: 0-89693-371-7

VICTOR BOOKS
A division of SP Publications, Inc.
        Wheaton, Illinois 60187

Contents

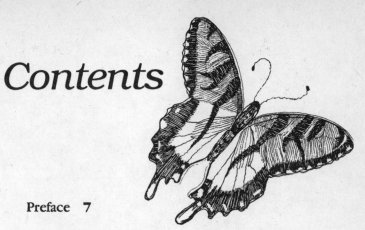

Preface

Lord,

All around us we see brokenness, and we are aware of the fragility of life.

There is a child's delicate trust and sense of wonder which can be so easily trampled and broken.

There is a teenager's sense of self-worth which can be completely shattered by a word or simply by a disapproving look.

There is a family's unit of love, respect, and closeness which can be marred by criticism or misunderstandings, dividing family members into torn and fragmented individuals.

There is a marriage (we all thought was so whole and sturdy) which can splinter into pieces before our eyes.

There is an old man, a young boy, and a middle-aged woman who all suffer from the crushing effects of daily pressures. Their minds are emotionally disturbed and frail.

O, dear Lord, be the glue that holds our fragmented hearts and minds together and never let us forget Your words:

"I am leaving you with a gift—peace of mind and heart! And the peace I give isn't fragile like the peace the world gives. So don't be troubled or afraid" (John 16:33, author's paraphrase).

Thank You, Lord, for that because these *are* very fragile times and sometimes we *are* afraid.

JOYCE LANDORF

It's Me, It's Me, O Lord, Standin' in the Need . . .

"I Tell You This in Love"

My hair has always been my own personal Waterloo. My husband finds it all very humorous that I can cook, sew, quilt, hook rugs, do yarn pictures, and play the piano, but cannot comb my hair. I don't find it a bit funny.

Once, due to a busy schedule before a musical concert, I fixed my own hair. After the concert I was really drained of strength, but I managed to stand and talk with people. Then *she* stood before me.

"My dear," she began, and I knew by the way she spoke that I was in for it. I braced myself for the next words, which I could almost hear before she said them. "I tell you this in Christian love." Since that remark is hardly ever followed by "I love you," I waited for her critical observations.

She didn't disappoint me. "How long have you been wearing your hair like that?" she asked.

"About three days," I answered.

"Well," she continued, "while you were singing,

the Lord told me you shouldn't wear it like that; you must definitely change it."

The reaction I felt was not too spiritual. In fact, the carnal Joyce would have gladly taken a poke at the old darling without batting an eyelash. But that very week the Lord had been dealing with me about my responsibility to love others—even the annoying ones.

I prayed silently, "Lord, it's simply not possible to love this lady. I'm tired, and she's meddling in my private business. I hate her sweet smile and her 'I tell you this in Christian love' when she's really speaking out of human meanness. I wonder which little ole lady said that to David before he wrote, 'Restore unto me the joy of Thy salvation' " (Ps. 51:12, KJV).

Though my prayer was quick and casual, the Lord heard and understood. Suddenly I really saw her. She was in her 70s, and, of all things, she was wearing a wig! Somehow it had slipped and was actually sitting sideways on her head. The picture of her with her ridiculous looks telling me about my hair struck me as the funniest thing I'd seen in a long time, and instantly my "joy of salvation" was completely restored.

I thanked her for her comments, promised to do something about my hair, and went away giggling.

Thank You, Lord. I really don't want my attitude to be as unmanageable as my hair.

The Right to Be Me

The voices are everywhere, and they all seem to be screaming for me to *be* something different from what I am.

They say that if I don't have an education, I should get my credentials. If I'm fat, I should be thin. If I'm a brunette, I should be a blond. And the obsession with change goes on.

It's not that I'm against change. I like how the fresh clean rain of spring clears the air and makes everything blossom. But I'm afraid we can miss the "now" of our lives by overemphasizng a need for change. The daily miracles that God provides can be lost in our everlasting quest for things "beyond our reach."

I have a right to be me. And you have the right to be you. However, some of the things we'd like to be might not be what God intends for us.

Actually, I think it would be super to be a Corrie ten Boom. But it's not God's plan for me to be anybody but me. And the sooner I accept the "who I am" God has made, the sooner the Holy Spirit can work at making me God's person.

An anonymous writer once declared the meaning of "being me" in very clear terms when she wrote:

"I hold no college degree, I'm not neurotic, I'm not frustrated, and I don't take tranquilizers. I'm your average run-of-the-mill wife and mother.

"I've never owned a Cadillac, but I've looked at the breathtaking scene of a winter sunset.

"I've never been to an opera, but I've listened to the songs of birds, the sounds of crickets, and the sighing of the winds in the pines.

"I've never received a standing ovation, but I've shared the miracle of creation and the thrill of hearing a tiny voice whisper, 'You're the best mother in the whole world.'

"Snow will fall in the winter; autumn will follow summer; leaves will drift aimlessly down as they have for centuries; my life shall cease. But I will not have lived and loved in vain.

"God chose me for this time and place. And if I had my life to live over, I would choose no other but do as I have done—asking the Holy Spirit to supply the strength and guidance for each day of my life."

Ephesians 1:4 reaffirms the right to be me—"according as He hath chosen us in Him before the foundation of the world, that we should be holy and without blame before Him in love" (KJV).

Thank You, Lord, for today, this moment, and the right to be me. Help me not to miss out on that miracle.

Beauty Secret

Yesterday I saw a beautiful woman. Her inner glow was quiet, like a small yellow buttercup; but that same inner glow was loud enough to sound like an explosion in a dynamite factory.

I watched as she talked with other people, how she laughed, how she hugged, how she listened, how she stood, caring so much. Then I realized her inner beauty was really an inner spiritual quality.

Oh, I don't mean pious, holy spirituality. I mean warm, loving, tender spirituality. I don't mean hypocritical spirituality. I mean honest, sincere, approachable spirituality.

Yesterday I saw a beautiful woman, and I thought, "No wonder no one can adequately define beauty. It's a fragrance, a God-given fragrance." With each smile she smiles, with each word she speaks, and with each tear she cries, I see God. I cannot put my finger on it exactly, but God shines in her.

The rare thing, though, is that she never clobbers

me with her spirituality. She does not throw in my face how she gets up early to pray and read Scripture each morning. She does not tell me who she is fasting for this week (or that she is even fasting, yet I think she is).

She did not leave one single mark of identification on the cupcakes left on my doorstep two days ago, yet I'm sure she brought them. She didn't ask me later if I enjoyed those cupcakes.

No, when I saw her yesterday, she didn't drive the steam roller of her spiritual achievements over my soul. She didn't in any way demand recognition or reward.

She is a woman who has taken the words of Jesus and made them her lifestyle. Her gifts to others, spiritual or material, are wholesome. I'm sure she has taken very much to heart our Lord's words:

"Take care! Don't do your good deeds publicly, to be admired, for then you will lose the reward from your Father in heaven. But when you do a kindness to someone, do it secretly—don't tell your left hand what your right hand is doing. And your Father who knows all secrets will reward you" (Matt. 6:1, 3-4).

Yesterday I saw a beautiful woman whom God, surely, is rewarding. And to us who stood beside her, the essence of her spirituality was incredibly fragrant.

Back
to School

I've reluctantly signed up for a new course in the school of life. I didn't ask to take the class; I was suddenly pressured into it. What I thought would take a few weeks has turned into a full semester. I've joined a host of others who must study firsthand the problems of prolonged physical pain.

The class sessions are a little irregular. Sometimes class begins at 2 in the morning, calling me sharply and noisily out of a deep sleep. Other times it slowly interrupts a friend's afternoon conversation. But if its hours are irregular, its message is not. Consistent pain takes few recesses.

Today when class was definitely in session I read from Proverbs: "You are a poor specimen if you can't stand the pressure of adversity" (24:10).

I thought, "O Lord, I don't want to be a poor specimen, but I'm weary and the pressures of pain are so constant."

The course is teaching me that pain is monstrously

conceited. Pain stamps its foot and demands all my attention. It's hard to decide if I should have baked or mashed potatoes for dinner because pain holds my mind all wadded up in its tightly closed fist.

Pain also teaches the waiting game. Wait for doctor's appointments. Wait for test results. Wait for the medicine to take effect. Wait to see if a new procedure will correct or change the problem.

Today my teacher gave an exam on patience. I passed—but not because I was smart and had graduated to some upperclassman level of maturity. Rather, because I went back to the text, found the right answer, and wrote it down:

"We are pressed on every side by troubles, but not crushed and broken. We are perplexed because we don't know why things happen as they do, but we don't give up and quit. We are hunted down, but God never abandons us. We get knocked down, but we get up and keep going" (2 Cor. 4:8-9).

At this writing, I'm still in class. I don't like it, but I know God is in control. I know the truth of hanging on, pressing forward, and running the race. I will not give up or quit. I am God's child, but that does not mean I can skip or cut the classes on pain, so . . .

I thank You, Lord,

For whatever this class will be teaching.

It's interesting to be this old and back in school again.

The semester is long, and I'm tired.

But Your loving arms of strength are longer.

Help me keep that in mind until I graduate.

Six Months Later

Both women had lost their husbands after 26 years of marriage.

This morning I listened to Ruth (that's not her real name) as she told me about her devastating loss. Her husband died six months ago. "I'm cut in half," she said.

Years of sharing everything from thoughts and ideas to toothpaste and the morning newspaper have come to a grinding halt for her. She must break old patterns, learn to walk and breathe on her own—an adjustment that is neither wanted nor easily accomplished.

This afternoon's mail brought a letter from Lois (not her real name either). She too wrote of her irreparable loss. Like Ruth, she lost her husband six months ago.

She writes that one morning she got up and went out to the kitchen. Propped up against the coffee pot was a note. It read: *Dear Lois, I am leaving you. I will not be back. Sorry. Bill.*

Except for his signature on the divorce papers, she had not seen him since. She never dreamed this could happen to them.

O Lord,
Two women have lost their husbands.
I do not understand the "whys" of either loss.
I find I am gentle, sympathetic, understanding,
and willing to bake cookies for one.
But for the other—
What can I say? What do I do?
She is half a person too, Lord.
Only it's hard to explain her loss to other couples,
  relatives, especially the children.

O Lord,
Both of these women are widows.
Give me a gentle compassion for them.
Not sticky sweet pity, but an open mind and a
  listening heart.
Help me not to prejudge the situation
  or hold myself up as a paragon of spiritual
  righteousness.
Breathe the right words for both women into my
  uncomprehending heart,
  for I don't know any brilliant, all-
  encompassing, and glorious answers.
Their needs, Lord, stun my ability to comprehend.

So I bring both women to You and thank You
  in advance for the healing which they both
  so desperately need.

Nothing Can Separate

I am convinced that nothing can ever separate us from His love. Death can't, and life can't. The angels won't, and all the powers of hell itself cannot keep God's love away. Our fears for today, our worries about tomorrow, or where we are—high above the sky, or in the deepest ocean—nothing will ever be able to separate us from the love of God demonstrated by our Lord Jesus Christ when He died for us (Rom. 8:38-39).

As a musician, I'm well aware of how very precious my piano is to me. For many years I've dreamed of owning a really great piano. This year my dream came true when we brought a Steinway grand piano into our living room. It's not a new one, but I lovingly care for it. I play it every day and keep it tuned and dusted.

The great violinist, Isaac Stern, once took his beloved instrument to a shop for some minor repairs. The shop owner invited Mr. Stern to watch as the craftsman fixed the broken part. The famous violinist is reported to have said, "Oh, no thank you, I'll wait out here until the operation is finished."

I smiled when I heard that story because I know how attached I am to my piano. I could understand Mr. Stern not wanting to be separated from his violin. Because his love for it was deep, he couldn't bear to watch the "surgery."

How very much we Christians are like the violin to the concert master in our relationship with the Lord: God, the Master, and we, His instruments. Only in our case the Lord made us and fashioned us out of nothing. Then He picked us up and by touching the strings of our lives brought forth fantastic music. Music out of sin and chaos, music out of confusion and fear. Music, glorious music.

His love for His instruments is so strong He will not be separated from us. He not only watches the surgery in our lives, but handles the healing as well. Nothing stops Him from loving.

Paul's wise, joyous words were like a song to me this morning. "Has God deserted us?" the apostle asks. Then the answer comes ringing back again and again. "No! Nothing can separate us from His love!"

On us, His instruments, God plays a song unending.
On us, He pours out His inexhaustible source of love,
and we in turn will never be separated from it.
    Lord, truly let us be Your usable instruments.

Bare Walls

We are moving from a house we've lived in 11 years. I must say, I'd forgotten all the hassles, fatigue, and just plain work moving brings with it.

Yesterday we took down all our pictures and boxed them. Then we packed the teacups that adorned the dining room hutch shelves. By evening the house seemed devoid of everything that says, "The Landorfs live, love, and laugh here." In one day we had stripped away our home's inner personality.

The house looked a little like me a number of years back. After I became a Christian, I knew if I died I'd go to be with the Lord; but a lot of things about me left much to be desired. I was like a house without furnishings.

There was precious little fruit-of-the-Spirit evidence of my Christianity. Oh, there was *some* love, joy, peace, patience, kindness, goodness, faithfulness, gentleness, and self-control. But overall, these things were in scarce supply.

The fruit of the Spirit have not come all at once to me, nor have they been even in their growth rate. It's more like getting one room of a new house done at a time; adding a picture or piece of furniture as the budget allows.

I've learned through the years—as a homemaker and a Christian—that keeping house is a full-time job. I can quickly see the results if I neglect my prayer life. I soon feel the effect if I don't study God's Instruction Book. I become a house stripped of personality and character. I am a house with nobody home.

O Lord, packing and moving is such a fatiguing job. But thank You for the glimpse of bare walls, empty cabinets, and a house void of "fruit," because I've seen myself a little clearer. How like this house I have at times become. How easy it is not to grow in love, joy, and kindness. How simple it is to sit back and not be known for all those delicious fruit of Your Spirit.

Lord, I need the work of the Holy Spirit in my life—constantly—so I will not be an empty house. Help me to remember this bare house the next time I'm tempted to be spiritually lazy. Jog my memory to action and get me hanging pictures and stuffing the cupboards of my soul with Your presence.

Let my house reveal that Somebody lives inside.

Conversation at 8:30 A.M.

My first cup of coffee
Sits before me, Lord.
There's so much to do, but
I need to stay here a bit longer
And talk with You.

The children are both off to school
Letting knowledge seep in
With varying degrees of success.

I care about grades, but more,
About knowledge.
I want them to be popular, but more,
To be strong of character.
Protect them today in their pressure-cooker world.

Frovide Your wisdom instead of man's intellectual
    theories.
And prepare them to be the steady adults

You want them to be.
They are Yours.

My second cup of coffee
Sits before me now.
My watch has erased
Ten more minutes from its face.
By now
My husband has successfully threaded
His way through traffic and
He sits at a desk marked by his name.
I'd like to talk to You about him.
He *seems* ready to fight the dragons
In his arena today.
But, Lord, if he's not *sure* it's worth it all,
Speak to him, please.

You know he takes his role of
Husband and father very seriously.
It could cause him ulcers.
Lord, he is a rare man. I love him.
What can I do for him?
I've tried
Getting up early and fixing his breakfast,
Ironing all his shirts at one time,
Fixing eggplant casserole with bacon,

Wearing the blue negligee,
Giving his back a great rub and
Pulling weeds out of the strawberries.
To no avail.
His shoulders still have that
Uptight-with-pressure look.
I guess, Lord, what he really needs
Is an *inner* kind of happening.
One I can only *ask* for—not give.

Like,
Lead him to the right person
    for some needed encouragement.
Help him to hear (or overhear)
    the exact comment to make him relax and smile.
(Actually, Lord, what he needs is a good laugh.)

Give him some concrete proof today,
To let him know his goals are being achieved.
Then do convince him that he is
Covered by his family's love and prayers.

See, only You and the Holy Spirit can give him
That kind of inner security.

Well, the last quarter inch of coffee
Is cold in my cup.
Lord, I've sat here too long, but, oh, it's been good
    to talk with You!

The
Marriage-
Go-Round

The Lost Word

If there is any word that has been dropped, lost, or fallen out of sight in the past decade, it's been the word *commitment.*

There seems to be very little commitment (or none at all) between

Husband and wife
Employer and employee
Employee and job
Teenager and parents
Parents and offspring
Politicians and government
Government and people

In fact, the attitude seems to be: Do your own thing and if it doesn't work out—quit!

A young couple just married three years state, matter-of-factly, "We feel nothing for each other. We are no longer in love, so we are getting a divorce." The word *commitment* never comes up and I wonder why. They asked each other to marry; no one forced them to; and now they have lost their "feeling of being in love," so their life together has to be terminated, they say.

I wish I had a nickel for all the times I did not *feel* such-and-such.

Like the time my children deliberately disobeyed me and in the angry outburst that followed broke my favorite cut-glass bowl. I did not *feel* like a loving, warm, understanding mother. However, nothing changed the position of my commitment. I was, am, and will always be a mother. Throwing in the sponge because I do not *feel* like a mother would be the biggest cop-out of the year.

There are times as a wife when I am not overwhelmed with loving thoughts toward my husband (and vice versa!), but that must not make us lose sight of our marriage commitment to each other.

There are dry times too in our lives when, spiritually, we *feel* God is far away. We lose sight of His overall plan and we miss, also, His generous blessed commitment to us.

The fifth verse of Psalm 31 came flooding into my day with a new brilliance this morning:

> Into Thine hand I *commit* my spirit: Thou hast redeemed me, O Lord God of truth (KJV).

David was not dying when he wrote that verse. He was voicing a prayer he may have prayed daily.

I've asked the Lord to ignore my feelings—for feelings are about as stable as a bouncing, rolling yo-yo—and to renew my commitment.

The word *commitment* needs to be written across my mind and heart so that when the going is rough or,

worse, invisible, I will not be tempted to give up and
quit. I will say, with the psalmist, "Into Thy hand, I
commit. . . . "
My spirit
My husband
My children
My work
My all.

Honesty
Is Expensive

It's painful for me to relive my five years of fear, failure, and frustration as a wife, mother, and woman. It costs to share the fact that, though I was raised in the church and had all the answers at my fingertips, I had to be actually attempting suicide before the Lord could reach me.

Not long ago as I was giving a live radio concert at a large church in San Jose, I was tempted to skip over my testimony and just sing. Yet, for God's reasons, I gave a very brief account of my marriage breakup and how a young minister phoned me just as I was putting the razor blade to my wrist.

Then I shared the glorious part about Christ coming to me that day. I ended with the song, "He Touched Me."

Soon afterward a friend wrote from San Jose. It seems that the Sunday I was there her neighbor had finalized plans to leave her husband, teenagers, and a 24-year marriage because her life with all of them was "over." She believed she'd never loved her husband and that the time had come to try to find something or someone else while she could.

Around 6 P.M. that day she packed her bags and left, intending never to return. On her way to oblivion, she stopped at a drugstore. A local radio station, blaring above the noisy ring of the cash registers, caught her attention. Some woman was telling over the air how her marriage had failed, how she had been about to take her life, and how God stepped in.

The deserting woman stood by a counter and listened. After the final song, she decided to give God her life and marriage. She went home and sought out some Christian neighbors. She is giving Christ her fears and needs today.

When my friend wrote me about all this, I realized how dangerously close I'd come to not sharing the rocky part of my life.

If for no other person than a heartbroken, defeated woman in an all-night drugstore, I'm glad I told my story over the air.

Sometimes we don't see miracles happening in our

lives, or in the lives of others, because we're afraid to risk being honest.

It *is* costly to be honest, to live where our talk is and to really share the Good News; yet the price Christ paid for us was far greater. And He never once cared about the cost.

Partners in Prayer

I wish I could tell you that right from the second my husband, Dick, and I became Christians we had a marvelous prayer life, but that's not the way it happened.

We were novices at praying separately, much less together. Fumbling and embarrassed as he was, praying out loud was essentially painful for Dick. My noisy nature allowed me a bit more freedom, but it was remarkable how easily Dick went to sleep while I prayed.

While Dick prayed, I found I could mentally redecorate the bathroom or let my mind wander to any number of projects. It's no wonder we soon lost interest in this boring concept of prayer.

We might have missed forever the most enriching time of our lives had it not been for a flight to San Francisco I took with Dr. Ralph Byron, a skilled surgeon who is equally adept at teaching a Sunday School lesson.

Dr. Byron was the speaker that night for a banquet in San Francisco, and I was to provide the special music. I remember sitting next to him on the plane, thinking, *I know he has a vital prayer life with Dorothy—but when?* He was in surgery before dawn every day and not out till afternoon. He scheduled many speaking engagements in the evening, yet I just knew he prayed with his wife. I was so sure of it, I blurted out, "Dr. Byron, just when do you and Dorothy pray?"

He smiled and answered, "Just before we go to sleep at night."

"But," I questioned, "doesn't one of you fall asleep before the other finishes?"

He turned in his seat, looked directly at me, and got to the heart of my probing with—"Ah, I see you and Dick are not praying the right way."

"OK, I give up. How do you pray the 'right way'?" I asked.

There on the plane, thousands of feet in the air, he gave me one of life's most valuable lessons on prayer. That lesson turned prayer sessions with Dick into the most beautiful times of our lives.

When I got home, I shook Dick out of a deep sleep. "Honey, I've got to tell you what Dr. Byron told me about prayer tonight."

Dick didn't wake up completely, but he was aware it was 2 A.M. and I was home safely from the airport. "Mm, that's nice, Honey; glad you're home. See you in the morning," he mumbled.

I pestered him into a wakeful but blurry-eyed awareness and he said, "OK, give me the plan and we'll take 10 minutes to pray, and then I'm going back to sleep."

Forty-five minutes later he said, in a surprised way, "Why did you stop so soon?"

Dr. Byron had suggested we take turns each night at being the leader or introducer of requests. This night it was my turn, and in one short sentence I introduced and prayed very conversationally for subject number one. Then Dick prayed a short sentence for subject one. Next I introduced and prayed on subject two and Dick followed. We repeated the process till we had covered about seven items.

The prayers had been so interesting, like talking with God in a three-way conversation, we'd completely lost track of time.

The next night it was Dick's turn to introduce the requests of his heart, and within a week several things began happening.

First of all, at dinner one night I said, "Well, how did it go at work today?"

Dick matter-of-factly answered, "Oh, just fine." But later that same night, after he introduced subject number four, he prayed, "Lord, help me to know how to handle George and the serious problems he's creating at the bank."

My first thought was, *For pete's sake—George who?* Then I realized what Dick could not talk about at the dinner table, or in conversation with me, he felt perfectly free to present to the Lord.

I remember praying intensely for old George what's-his name that night and being just thrilled that Dick had mentioned a real need in his life.

Next, we noticed that on my night to introduce, I'd pray for Dick's requests. On Dick's night, many of my concerns would show up on his list. The bond of love grows deep when we see our partner caring, remembering, and praying for our needs and requests.

I'll never get over the first time, on my husband's night to introduce, he ended by praying, "Lord, thank You for my dear wife, I love her so much. Give her a good night's sleep and a great day tomorrow."

If, after so many years of marriage, you can fall in love all over again with the same person, that was the moment for me. How strange it was: There we were praying together because we knew we should (almost like a duty); but suddenly we found ourselves, because of prayer, falling deeply in love with each other.

I remember quiet tears streaming down my face in the darkness that night. Telling God how grateful he was for me and that he loved me was the most romantic thing my husband had ever done.

If I could wave a magic wand for you in regard to your prayer life, I'd wish several things:

1. Make time, in the ideal place, for conversational prayer with your spouse. It need not always be the same amount of time—your needs differ from day to day—but take whatever time you need. It's important to keep vertical channels open to God as well as horizontal communication between each other.

2. Keep requests simple, honest, and liberally sprinkled with genuine thankfulness.

3. Listen to each request with all your hearing abililty. You may pick up clues to your partner's emotional and spiritual temperature. You may hear more than verbal intonations, and this may be one of the best ways for you to understand the other's inner tickings. (You know, those which are such a mystery to you.)

4. Ask God to give you a keen sensitivity to know when to drop everything and right-then-and-there

pray aloud. I mean this for your partner's and your children's prayer lives as well.

5. Be real in your praying. Your spouse needs to hear you pray honestly—from your heart. Your partner needs to see you cry over the heartaches of people around you, and, most of all, to feel your love for God. All this can be accomplished through your praying together.

6. Before you pray, check out your attitude and treatment of your wife or husband. Peter, that outspoken individualist and rugged fisherman, suggests rather strongly that, if a man is having trouble praying and his prayers aren't too effective, he should examine how he is treating his wife. It's surprising to read Peter's subtle yet blunt pronouncement: "You husbands likewise, live with your wives in an understanding way, as with a weaker vessel, since she is a woman; and grant her honor as a fellow-heir of the grace of life, so that your prayers may not be hindered" (1 Peter 3:7, NASB).

The blessings in your life can depend on how you treat your companion in life.

Reprinted by permission from *Tough, and Tender* by Joyce Landorf, © 1975, Fleming H. Revell Company, Old Tappan, New Jersey.

Battleground
or Sanctuary?

As I read Ephesians 2:14-16 recently, my eyes did a funny thing. I knew Paul was talking about two groups of people (Jews and Gentiles), but my eyes kept reading my name and my husband's name every time I looked at it. It read something like this:

"For Christ Himself is our way of peace. He has made peace between Dick and Joyce by making us all one family, breaking down the wall of contempt that used to separate us.... Then He took Dick and me, who had been opposed to each other, and made us parts of Himself; thus He fused us together to become one new person, and at last there was peace. As parts of the same body, our anger against each other has disappeared, for both of us have been reconciled to God. And so the feud ended at the cross" (adapted, TLB).

I love the line, "Both of us have been reconciled to God." I'd like to hear and be reminded of that in every wedding ceremony, because that's the starting point for a great Christian marriage.

We can actually become agents of reconciliation because of this right standing with God.

I remember, before we were Christians, how our home was a highly defined battleground. Now, after Christ, it's more like a sanctuary.

Before, both my husband and I were talented disrupters. Now, after Christ, we are gentle healers. Not because we "try harder," but because of Christ's work in our hearts.

The Lord broke us. And it was the Lord who built (slowly) the bridge of reconciliation that connects us. We are not only connected together, but with Him as well.

Read and personalize Ephesians 2:14-16 sometime this week. Then tuck it away in your memory and someday, when small but threatening details mar your marriage and family life, go take another look at what God has really done for you.

Recalling this passage will add to your thankful spirit. You will be able to thank the Lord, then tackle the problem the right way—head-on.

Ask yourself what picture your children will carry into adulthood of your family life. How will they remember you? Will they picture their home as a battleground or as a sanctuary? Will they long remember you as as disrupter or a healer?

We are to be agents of reconciliation. In the home *first.* Then out into the world.

"No Occupation"

In filling out all sorts of cards or information reports, the space that's marked *Occupation* seems to give women the most frustration.

If you are a working wife and mother, you fill in the words, "dental assistant," "teacher," "librarian," "waitress," or whatever in the little space. But if you are not employed outside the home, what do you write?

Just recently, for a credit card at our local grocery store, I wrote "Housewife" beside *Occupation.*

"That's *not* what we want," the manager said. "We don't consider housewife an occupation. We mean an outside-the-home job."

I wish the words, "full-time wife and mother" would be upgraded a bit. This occupation has been given such a royal put-down that a lot of women who have chosen wifehood (and all its implications) feel ridiculously unworthy. When asked what they do for a living, they answer in a dreary tone of voice, "I'm just a housewife."

Yet many of us, by our own choice, have opted for marriage—its hassles, its joys, its children, and (at times) its dull routine. We have a right to be full-time, part-time, or some-time as the Lord directs in our lives. We need not feel ashamed or guilty in our decision.

In my own life (with God's help and my husband's full consent) I have been privileged to be both, a working wife and a housewife. While speaking and singing have taken their share of time, my real joy has come as a homemaker.

Enjoying the traditions of a housewife begins with attitudes. If we women are ashamed of our inside-the-home job, if we feel it's beneath our talents, or if we're mad at being there, we will probably *never* make a success of our lives.

However, if we ask God for a priority list and He clearly tells us, "1. Husband, 2. Children, *then* 3. Outside job," we can arrange our attitudes to fit the plan very well. We women are fantastic at looking a challenge straight in the eye and accepting it.

The woman in Proverbs 31 knew exactly where her

priorities were. No one dared question her loyalty to her husband or her service to her children. She showed remarkable steadfastness to her housework, yet she maintained a business in the marketplace and did a little moonlighting in real estate properties.

I have a hunch, had she filled out an information card, she would have proudly written by *Occupation*: "Housewife—and Glad of It!"

"Who can find a virtuous woman? For her price is far above rubies" (Prov. 31:10, KJV).

The Mother-in-Law Trap

If you throw the word *mother-in-law* to a group of people you get the best mixer, break-the-ice game going in the world. Everyone has something to say about his or her mother-in-law.

Our society has stereotyped the mother-in-law as meddlesome, destructive, and interfering. Yet for every bad mother-in-law I hear about, I know three or four who are marvelous.

The reason I've been thinking, studying, and observing mothers-in-law lately is that in less than three months I'm going to be one. In order to prepare for the event and not to fall into any trap, I've asked the Lord to teach me all He can about being the very best of mothers-in-law.

He took me first to the Book of Ruth and showed me Naomi. Now *there* was a terrific mother-in-law! After reading the whole beautiful story again, I saw how very strong Naomi and Ruth's friendship was. I want such a loving, secure friendship. It certainly didn't "just happen" or "just keep going," but was carefully nurtured and cared for meticulously.

Next, the Lord gave me a "guideline" verse for the years ahead in mother-in-lawing. I shall repeat it and apply it daily. "Be kind to each other, tenderhearted, forgiving one another, just as God has forgiven you because you belong to Christ" (Eph. 4:32).

Finally, the Lord had me take a good long look at our own son and our about-to-be daughter. He showed me an instant replay of the 20 years our son has been with us and how God's hand has guided. Then He showed me our son's choice of a helpmeet, and I knew God had her in mind all along. She's wonderful.

The Lord pointed out that the matrimonial road ahead is filled with difficult years of study. (He wants to be a missionary doctor and she is halfway toward a teaching degree.) Their financial and material cupboards will be quite bare, but the Lord assured me they are rich in His love, power, and wisdom.

My responsibility as a mother-in-law boils down to three lovely things:

1. I will lift them to the throne of God daily.
2. I will be available anytime they need me.
3. I will accept them as they are. God made them and they are His children.

If you see any tears glistening in my eyes the night of the wedding, they will only be tears of joy. In fact, I have so much of the Lord's deep settled peace about letting our son go, I think I'll help him pack.

"You'll Like Shirley"

The agency that handles all the booking arrangements for my speaking and singing also represents Dr. James Dobson, author of many best-selling Christian books.

Some time ago we agreed, that in addition to our individual appearances, Dr. Dobson and I would take on a team ministry using the seminar techniques for couples. The two of us met many times to discuss plans and an instant rapport was formed between the doctor and me.

Since I had not met his wife, Shirley, and he had not been introduced to my husband, Dick, we decided to spend an evening at home together to get acquainted.

For our work to have some degree of success in helping families and marriages, I felt our personal relationships with our mates and families must not only be right, but healthy and loving.

As usual, I was very pressed for time (and Dr. Dobson was hard to reach by phone), so I simply dropped him a note asking if he and Shirley could come for dinner that week or next.

Dr. Dobson found it equally hard to reach me, so he wrote a short letter in reply. I'll always be grateful I couldn't be phoned because that would have cheated me out of one extraordinary line in his letter.

His first page was all about the new house they had needed, found, and purchased. He thanked me for our prayers on this matter, as it had worked out very well. Then the next page began:

"We are getting unpacked now and would be delighted to join you for dinner sometime next week. How would the 14th or 15th be? I'm looking forward to meeting your family. And you'll like Shirley."

The following line jumped right off of the page at me: "She's my best friend."

Those few words told me just about everything concerning their marriage, their mutual love, and deep respectful trust for each other. Their Spirit-controlled attitudes and their own self-worth and acceptance of each other was clearly visible.

Our evening together was one of the most beautiful and rare evenings we've ever had. Christ, reflected in both of those beautiful people, warmed us and all the rooms in our home.

If someone were to ask you right now, "What sentence best describes your relationship with your mate?" I wonder what you would answer. Would you be able to say, "She's (or he's) my best friend"?

They Need a Miracle

I was disturbed about the note that was being slipped from person to person down the front row of choir one Sunday morning. When it reached me, I was even more chagrined. It had my name on the outside. Feeling guilty, I opened it to read:

"See the couple on the fifth row in the west auditorium aisle seats? He has on a navy blue suit with a pale blue shirt and she is dressed in lavender."

I counted rows, found the blue shirt, and saw a handsome but terribly solemn couple. Then I read on:

"Their marriage is over. Pray for them—they need a miracle." The note was unsigned.

I began to concentrate on loving and praying for this couple who "needed a miracle." Both of them sat terribly attentive, facing the pastor; but an expression, smile, or nod never altered their faces as they played the game of "let's pretend we are in church."

As I sat there praying that morning, two things

Jesus said were very clearly established in my mind:

1. Jesus asked us to love one another (John 15:12). He did not confine it to people we know and love, but to "one another."

2. Jesus said that nothing is impossible (Matt. 19:26). That note said the couple's marriage was over, but no one knows any better than Dick and Joyce Landorf that God can take an "over" marriage and miraculously make it alive again.

After I'd committed the troubled couple to God, I wondered about the people seated behind and to the left of them. Did they need a miracle too? It seemed to me that I'd wasted some prime praying time during my years of sitting in the choir loft.

The next Sunday during processionals, offering, and other breaks, I looked for people needing miracles. I prayerfully asked the Lord which ones were the most needy. It's been a rich experience and the Lord has produced some real growth in my own life.

I may never know what happened to the couple I first prayed for. They returned for the next three Sundays, but I've not seen them since. I've wondered if they got their much needed miracle. Only the Lord knows just where those two unhappy people are today. I've entrusted them, wherever they are, into His keeping.

In the meantime, I've picked out an older couple who sit off to my right and three junior high girls in the balcony to ask the Lord for an impossible miracle for whatever they might need.

We Hold
Our
Children
with
Open Arms

Dad's Hand

For three winters and summers of my life, my father pastored a church in Owen Sound, Ontario. My memory bank is stuffed with warm recollections of those years.

Of course, when you're only eight years old you see everything larger than life. The summers and the flowers were brighter and better than any place in the world. The Georgian Bay water was bluer than any blue had a right to be. The winters were snowier and prettier than any Christmas card ever depicted.

Sometimes in winter we walked to church on Sundays. Instead of driving along a river and crossing a bridge, we'd walk across the river on ice.

The first time we'd do it in December both frightened and excited me. My eager, joyous jumping up and down was instantly quashed the moment we stepped off the bottom step of the dock and took our first slidy steps onto the ice. Dark rings of slushy ice and water surrounded the big ships on either side of the river. Where we stood seemed safe enough, with thick, firm white ice underfoot. But the terrible blackness around those ships terrified me.

I would never have crossed the frozen path if my father, in loving confidence, had not said, "Joyce, take my hand and walk with me. If you stay right by me, you'll be all right."

And so, hesitantly, I put my little red mitten in his big brown leather glove and we began our daring journey. There was something so sure, so confident in my father's strides and manner that almost immediately I lost my terror. The walk turned into an adventure.

I did a lot of sliding and twirling, pretending I was an ice skating queen. How bold and brave I was! How joyous and free I acted—all because Daddy held my hand.

Today, I discovered something dark and forbidding in my life. With a sudden jolt of recognition, I understood that I needed to reach up and take my heavenly Father's hand. The dark thing still scares me a bit, but my hand is inside a larger one.

My heavenly Father is not discouraged. He is not afraid. He is to be trusted. He will not shove me into waters that are deep and over my head. He walks firmly, confidently, and so can I.

I am happy even in the presence of dark things, for my trembling fingers are safely enclosed in His steady hand.

"He fills me with strength and protects me wherever I go" (Ps. 18:32).

Why the Hurt, Lord?

It's been eight years since our baby son David died. You'd think I'd be completely over his death by now, wouldn't you?

But yesterday in the park, when I saw a blond, blue-eyed boy about eight years old trying to get his kite aloft, I remembered David and the hurt was fresh and painful.

He was with us for such a brief flash in time that my hurt is not nearly so deep as a mother's who has 15 or 20 years of memories with a child before he is taken. Yet I think a bereaved mother will always yearn and miss the little one that slipped away.

I've been thinking and wondering about the *whys* of yesterday's hurt, and I've come up with three ideas.

Maybe one of the best reasons God allows us to remember a pinprick of grief from time to time has to do with His developing *awareness* in us.

Losing David gave us a new vital awareness toward our other son and daughter. It seemed to put a new light on them and our ability to appreciate them became razor sharp.

Another reason God allows the hurt seems to be in connection with the word *empathy.*

Having walked in the shadows of death's valley, I can reach out to a friend in his grief. I can silently and wordlessly cross the bridge of love toward him. We need no words, for my empathy is strong.

One more reason for the heartache to linger concerns our *understanding.*

Yesterday in the park, when I saw the boy, I asked the *why* of David's going for the hundredth time and patiently God answered (for the hundredth time):

"My child, stop asking, 'Why did You do that, Lord?' and ask, 'What do You want me to learn from this?' I want to teach you many things. Death is a vital part of life. I've allowed you to experience this sorrow to refine your living. You are My child; I am in control, even in David's death, and I will continue to direct your path. Trust Me, dear child."

I left the park and the boy without a backward glance. I was filled with a quiet, peaceful joy and I smiled as the verse popped gently into my thoughts—

"Since the Lord is directing our steps, why try to understand everything that happens along the way?" (Prov. 20:24)

It Doesn't Just Happen

Motherhood has been exploding all around me lately!

The dog of a family we know recently gave birth to 10 puppies. And Laurie, as she dashed out the front door, startled a brown sparrow off her nest under the roof eaves. Then a cat we were taking care of gave birth to 5 kittens in one of our closets.

As Laurie and I watched the cat have her kittens, I was struck by the orderly, tidy procedure she followed. The cat was a study in motherhood as she did whatever had to be done at just the right moment—even though it was her first litter.

A coincidence? Hardly. I'm sure she waited for her God-given instincts to direct her activities. She did cry out in pain each time a kitten was born, but quickly resumed her birth-giving duties.

I kept thinking of the wonder of it all. Who told her to find a cramped, tiny place in a closet so she could push against the wall when she needed leverage? Who taught her to take short, panting breaths? Who instructed her about the severing of the umbilical cord, the disposing of the placenta, and the cleaning of each kitten?

I guess what I'm really saying is, I could never be an atheist. To suggest that all I saw just happens without divine planning is too farfetched. In fact, I think it takes more faith to be an atheist than it does to believe in God.

My mind can grasp the idea that God created life far better than it can accept that something plus something accidentally came together to create such an amazing world.

God did create and is in control of all the universe. We didn't just happen or evolve. No, it had to be planned by a Supreme Being with an awesome creative ability.

"The heavens declare the glory of God; and the firmament showeth His handiwork" (Ps. 19:1, KJV).

Not only do the heavens declare God's glory, but the little living things, like the cat and her kittens, do as well. How wonderful God is!

Before writing this, I found out that our son, Rick,

and daughter-in-law, Teresa, would be having a baby. I would be a grandmother for the first time.

My grandchild's birth will give me another opportunity to observe, firsthand, God's creative abilities.

No, motherhood doesn't just happen. It's part of God's wonderful plan for the whole world!

Immaturity vs. Defiance

Two weeks after giving birth to five kittens in my closet, our neighbor's cat died. We were left to care for the helpless but playful babies. During that time I learned the difference between immaturity and defiance in both kittens and children.

For instance, the kittens would pay no heed to my warnings when I caught them shredding the newspaper on the floor. To kittens, tearing things is part of growing up. You can't tell a kitten not to use its claws

or ramble uncontrollably around the house. That is a kitten's nature. You shouldn't try to make a year-old-cat out of a five-week-old kitten.

The same kittens, however, knew that climbing up on the kitchen sink was wrong. But they would still do it in defiance of me. They knew they were wrong. All I would have to do was clear my throat and they would scatter.

How the kittens knew the difference between defiance and immaturity is a mystery to me. But I soon learned that children have the same nature.

One day, while grocery shopping, I noticed a young mother who had grown impatient with her young son. "Why don't you stand still!" she snarled.

I thought, *The word "still" doesn't exist in a child's vocabulary. All he knows are words like "jump," "move," "bang," and "shake."*

When her child didn't stand still, the mother demanded, "Why don't you grow up?"

I thought, *That's exactly what he's doing. The only problem is that it takes 20 years to grow a 20-year-old son.*

That is when I thought about the lesson I'd learned from watching the kittens' behavior. Though a child's behavior is more advanced than a kitten's, they're still similar. Both do things out of defiance or immaturity.

I looked at the young mother and remembered the times, when I was her age, that I made the same mistake of not distinguishing between my children's moments of immaturity and their times of defiance. I usually treated both as defiance.

I think we should expect and accept things like restlessness from our children in their growing-up years. A kitten wouldn't be normal if it didn't sometimes break things while at play; and a child wouldn't be normal if his or her behavior resembled that of an adult.

Through the Holy Spirit, Christian parents have the power to be patient and understanding about the natural behavior of children. He also gives us the insight to know when a child is being defiant.

So help your children grow up normally by not punishing them for behavior that is natural, yet disciplining them for behavior that is defiant of what they know is right.

"The Fourth 'R'"

I remember Laurie's first days at kindergarten vividly, even if it was many years ago. I guess I'll never forget the weeks preceding the "big day" when Laurie finally went to school.

She was up before dawn each morning yanking the covers from around my neck and impatiently pulling me out of bed.

We made a strange sight then. She would run ahead, dragging me by the hand with various admonishments of "Hurry up, please, Mother!" while just about all the other kids were hanging behind their mothers, acting as if their legs were made of wood.

"Well, how did your day go?" I asked my breathless daughter (she ran all the way home).

"Oh, I really like school!" she pronounced.

I was going to ask her what her teacher said, but she'd already launched her report.

"And my teacher said we're going to learn the four Rs." I'd heard of three, but not four, so I held up four fingers and questioned her with my look.

"Yes, four Rs,—reading, 'riting, 'rithmatic, and right lines."

"That fourth one sounds special, Laurie, is it?" I asked.

"Oh, yes. It's the most important 'R' there is," she replied.

"How does it work?"

"Well," she grew confidential and serious, "it's very important to do what Teacher tells you, and when she says 'line up,' she means it. But you have to pay attention, because you might stand in the wrong line."

"Is that bad?" I asked.

"That's terrible," she said emphatically. "When Teacher says line up, you have to be in the right line or you're in trouble."

About that time our cat Tabby came in, and the two of them had a joyous reunion. Our talk ended, but my thoughts lingered as I went into the kitchen.

While I made dinner, I thought about the right lines. It was up to my husband and me to lay down the "right lines" for Laurie.

The psalmist wrote, "Show me Thy ways, O Lord; teach me Thy paths" (Ps. 25:4, kjv).

I held up those "right lines" and asked for God's blessings.

My thoughts were interrupted by the sound of Laurie's voice, "Know why it's really important to get into the right lines, Mom?"

"Tell me," I said, though I knew she would.

"Well, today, Billy wasn't paying attention to Teacher and he ended up in the line that went to the girl's bathroom!"

Ah yes. The four Rs. Thank You, Lord, for the lesson that day, because after all those years, You did lead Laurie into Thy paths and right lines.

The Web of Fear

Laurie was about nine years old when her fear of spiders really took over. She seemed able to cope with it during the day and even got so she could objectively examine a specimen without becoming completely unnerved, but at night it was another story!

Each evening she would sleep for one or two hours, then the nightmares would begin. I'd rush into her room to find her sitting or kneeling in bed, frantically brushing thousands of imaginary spiders and ants out of the sheets and blankets. Putting the light on and showing her the empty bed was some comfort, but fear had so emotionally exhausted her that returning to sleep was almost impossible.

Week after week, her screaming woke the entire family, and all of us began suffering fatigue from those disastrous nightmares.

Finally, after six weeks of interrupted rest, she screamed out in the night and I ran to her room for the umpteenth time. This time I did not turn on her bedroom light. I simply prayed—in a strong, commanding voice:

"Dear Lord, please take these spider dreams away from Laurie right now and give her good dreams instead. Thank You, Lord, for the good dream she is going to have. Amen."

With that, I tucked the blanket under Laurie's chin, kissed the little freckle on her nose, and went to bed.

I was putting bread into the toaster the next morning when a cheery voice behind me said, "Guess what!" When I turned, there stood Laurie all smiles. "I had the best dream *ever!* I dreamed you gave me 25¢ and said, 'Go to the candy store and buy whatever you want.' "

About a month later, I realized I'd been sleeping the whole night through. "Laurie," I asked, "are you having any more spider nightmares?"

"Nope," she answered.

"Did they all go away, completely?" I questioned.

"Not all at once," she said. "A couple of nights after you prayed for me, I woke up from a spider dream. I was going to call you, but instead I just prayed, *Dear Lord, take this dream away and give me the good kind,* and He did, so I didn't wake you."

The faith that God could take care of a real fear (even a subconscious one) made our Laurie a shining, sparkling little girl that morning. I'll never forget how beautiful and how rested and relaxed she looked. Prayer works!

From *The Fragrance of Beauty* by Joyce Landorf, © 1973, Victor Books, Wheaton, Ill.

"Glad I'm Home"

When Laurie turned 14, she went from sweet to sour overnight. Fortunately, her adolescent rebellion wasn't like that of many of her peers, who turned to drugs, alcohol, or ran away. She simply stayed home and gave us all fits!

She *hated* everything I wore. Each new skin eruption on her face was treated as a national disaster. She *knew* she was ugly, repulsive, and hopeless in personality and inner character.

Since she was a perfectly darling girl and we were "perfectly darling" parents, we had no idea what had hit us.

A few months before Laurie's 16th birthday, I insisted that she go on an Easter choir tour. She was furious at my insistence, but she went (grumbling all the way). I slipped a note into her suitcase: "We love you. We are praying for you."

While on the tour Laurie sent this postcard to her surprised parents: "Thanks so much for the note I found in my suitcase. If ever I needed you to pray for me, it's *got* to be now. I'm scared to sing tonight because there are so many things about God I'm not sure of. Maybe I haven't really taken God down from my 'shelf.' I guess He can be real."

Toward the end of the tour He did become real to her. We knew *something* had happened because she came in the front door, smelled my dinner cooking and said, "Mmmmm, what smells so good, Mom?" The shock was almost too great for me to answer.

A month later we found this note on our bed:

Mom and Dad,

This was a year I made 'being parents' very hard for you. I'm sorry for all the hurt I have caused. I have finally realized how much you both mean to me and how much I really love you.

I guess you can say I'm asking for forgiveness. I have asked God for forgiveness, but yet inside I don't feel forgiven. I realize I have to ask you for forgiveness so I can forgive myself and make God's forgiveness complete.

I still am unable to share with you the feelings and emotions I had on the tour or all the feelings of the last four months, but please be patient with me. Sometime I will be able to put the feelings into words.

Mom, I'm glad to be home again. I feel safe.

I share this with all you parents who are terribly sure your children will never make it. Laurie is now a beautiful, mature woman. We have watched God capture her whole being and really shine through her. God is definitely answering her prayers—not to mention ours!

In Charge
of Choices

She flung herself through our front door. "I told them
my mother wouldn't let me go see it!" she shouted
angrily at me.

*O dear Lord, she's still so young, this beautiful
daughter of ours.*

*I guess about all I know is that someday I'll have
to answer to You about her.*

*I can't let her go to this movie, Lord—it's not a
family film. It's more. Much more. Terribly
more.*

I'd love to please her.

I'd like to give in, even though I've said no.

I love her so.

*I'd like to grant her whatever her dear little
heart wants.*

But can I and still answer to You?

*In five more years we will reach our 20-year mark
together.*

Then she'll be doing the choosing on her own.
She'll be making the decisions.
But for now, O Lord,
Keep me strong while I'm "in charge of choices."
Help me not to become so stiff and rigid
That I snap with brittleness,
Not so soft that I bend in any direction like a
*   wet noodle,*
But keep me supple and pliable,
Able always to move in Your direction.
Lord, I can't drag our daughter through Your gates
*   by her hair.*
Guide me in providing the best decisions
So I can post all the right road signs along the
*   way.*

As to this film—O Lord,
I think it's far too heavy for her to carry.
Right now at this age, she needs to grow
And to be stronger before she tries out her
*   carrying ability.*
She's in her room now
Still mad at me I expect,
But nevertheless You have put me
*   "in charge of choices."*

You were right about me,
Darling daughter.
I won't let you go see *that* movie.
But, then,
You already knew in your heart of hearts
And I think you were counting on it.

Teenage Memo

If there is one thing rougher than being a teenager— it's having one.

Every mistake parents make usually comes up to hit them head-on during their children's teen years. Even for parents who have done almost everything right, their teenager can still drop out, rebel, or refute everything they believe in.

Most authorities agree that the best advice for parents or teen leaders is to try to see life as teenagers see it.

Recently I saw a list of reminders from a teenager to his parents. It was anonymous, and I suspect it was written by an adult. However, here are a few of the suggestions. They are very real, very down to earth; and they may help you see life from a teenager's viewpoint.

1. Don't spoil me. I know I shouldn't have all that I ask for. I'm really testing you.

2. Don't be afraid to be firm with me. I can

respect your firmness if it's fair.

3. Don't let me form bad habits. You may see them early, so tell me.

4. Don't correct or embarrass me in front of other people.

5. Don't protect me from the consequences of my behavior. I need to learn the painful way sometimes.

6. Don't forget that while I'm growing I cannot explain myself too well. The words I yell may not be what I really mean. You may have to listen from your heart—not your ears.

7. Don't be inconsistent. It really confuses me and disturbs my faith in you.

8. Don't tell me my fears are silly. They are all too terribly real.

9. Don't put me off when I ask what seems to be a dumb question. If you don't answer me, I'll seek answers elsewhere.

10. Don't think you are too spiritual or mature to apologize to me. An honest apology makes me feel surprisingly warm toward you.

11. Don't forget that I love experimenting and changing my mind. Please put up with each phase. I need to work things out.

12. Don't forget you are responsible for my Christian training. Please continue to show God to me by the way you live.

I pray these 12 rules will give you some extra insights into coping with the teenagers you're concerned about. I add one more thought to the list:

13. Don't ever think your love, prayer, and training are not worth it. They are.

We Laughed Together

Dave was 14 when his radiant, young Christian mother died suddenly of cancer. He was 16 when he became a member of the Sunday School class my husband and I co-taught.

Each Sunday he systematically blew our class and teaching efforts right out the door. So, naturally, my husband and I tackled him as our special project.

We began by deciding we'd try never to lose our sense of humor in class or with him, no matter how he challenged us. Next, we stood firm about our faith and what God's Word said. We knew the one hour on Sunday was too short a time span, so we asked Dave and a friend to come to Sunday dinners.

Dave was the kind of problematic teaching challenge you might get once in a lifetime. My husband and I learned much because of this boy; we were discouraged more because of this boy, but we laughed and loved beyond our abilities because of him.

I think I know the exact moment that Dave became our friend and we began to be able to teach him. I'd asked him to help me replant our front yard. At one point that afternoon, he stopped digging, looked studiously at me and said, *"Now* I know why I like you! You've got a sense of humor like my mother had."

The rest of the afternoon he talked about his joyous, fun-loving mother and how after she died he'd tried to find Christians with that same joy, but he'd given up. He'd found only critical and somber men and women of the faith. He had decided all Christians were that way, and he was in open rebellion against them.

After his first few weeks in our Sunday School class, he decided to test us to see if we'd lose the joy. (I didn't tell him, but he almost succeeded!) Then when we invited him to dinner, even after he'd broken up class a few times, he began to let us love him.

Now that he's grown we are still friends, and I'm sure we always will be, for we are still laughing.

A word to discouraged Sunday School teachers:

I always find it a little scary to remember how close Dave made us come to throwing in the towel of teaching. We came terribly close to losing our sense of humor and to missing God's teaching purposes.

Dave holds us personally responsible for being the only two people who showed him God's consistent love during his rebellious years. *We* almost missed and gave up the glorious challenge. *You* carry on, dear teacher!

Memory Building

What memories are you building for your children to carry into adulthood? As parents, we're continually programming a bank of traditions, ideals, and concepts which become memories for our children. Memories that will affect the way they think and live.

There are many opportunities for building special memories into the lives of your family, but here are three you might want to check yourself on:

1. *What are mealtimes like?*

The dinner hour is when, miraculously, most families are together in one room for more than a few minutes. Don't miss it! It's the best time to find out what's happening, to check progress on school or dating; and it's perfect for taking your family's emotional and spiritual temperature.

It requires good food, candlelight, dandelions (if no florist is available), the "no-knock policy," and some thoughtful questions. Save your disciplining and the day's batch of bills and bad news till dinner is over. And remember the no-knock policy not only applies to the kids, but to you and Dad as well.

Jesus made something special out of breaking bread with others, and we should catch the significance of eating together too.

2. *Am I really kind to my mate?*

One of the most ignored verses in the Bible is, "Be ye kind one to another" (Eph. 4:32, KJV). We tend to think of it only in broad general terms when it's really about a one-to-one relationship.

Your children will not only pick up ugliness, impatience, and anger because of your unkindness, but they'll also store up bad memories for life—and likely have the same attitudes. Replace these attitudes with kindness.

3. *Are our top priorities prayer, Bible reading, church attendance, and Christian fellowship?*

Our children's concept of God, the church, and other Christians clearly depends on where we place their importance in the home.

The story of Samuel and the priest Eli is a powerful illustration of priorities. It's the story of a mother's high spiritual priority which helped turn Samuel into a man of God. However, there is also the sad story of Eli and his low priority on spiritual things which cost him his sons, and eventually his life (1 Sam. 1—2; 4:11-18). In both cases, it was a matter of right or wrong priorities.

As parents, we're in charge of the fine art of constructing memories for our children. We need to keep the right priorities. May God help us not to miss or mess up the adventure.

For Those Encamped About Us

Hard-of-Hearing

Just yesterday I read some statistics which proved what I already knew: the noise level in your house (and mine) is highest in the kitchen.

Much of my time as a wife and mother is spent in that noisy chamber. Because of the high decibel count, I'm sure I'm getting a little hard-of-hearing.

As I think of it, most of the important decisions of our marriage have been reached as my husband leaned against the sink to talk with me.

The children's big, bigger, and biggest questions have often been asked while they were doing the dishes or fixing a snack.

Personally, I've never reminded the Lord about my need for His wisdom quite so much as before my kitchen stove.

Today I prayed:

Lord, I think I've just figured out why You have to shout so loudly at me. I'm spiritually hard-of-hearing. The noise level of the tensions and problems here in my kitchen have dulled my sensitivity to Your voice.

> *My ears have grown accustomed to the din of*
> > *families,*
> > *freeways,*
> > *working,*
> > *cleaning,*
> > *questions, and*
> > *phones.*

I think I need a hearing aid, one that's really turned up, or maybe I need a short time to withdraw from my kitchen and spiritually recharge my batteries.

Otherwise, I'll miss the sound of
> *a friend hurting,*
> *a daughter crying,*
> *a co-worker failing,*
> *a husband hurting, or*
> *a neighbor rejoicing.*

Lord, I don't want to miss anything! But there's a tremendous amount of interference going on down here, so please wash the apathy of indifference out of the inner place of my soul, remove the air-hammer voice of Satan, heal the infection of bitterness, and soothe the harshness of sounds with Your warm, fragrant balm of Gilead oil before I drown in this sea of ugly noise.

It's only four words, but it takes a long time to memorize: "Be still and know." Lord, let Your whisper come through. I don't want to miss anything!

a

's a New World Coming
ne forgetfulness of Christians. He say uffer from short memories."

I think he is too soft on me, as a Christian. Too often I've been guilty of forgetting what God has done in the past. A current crisis hits, and I suffer—not from a "short memory"— but from total amnesia.

My crisis wipes out all memories of what God has done in the weeks and months behind me. Then, for weeks ahead, I stumble around in the fog of spiritual amnesia.

The presence of the Holy Spirit seems to disappear from my life; my prayer and Bible study times are dry, unexciting experiences.

I was comforted this week as I realized that the Psalmist David suffered a bad attack of amnesia at least on one occasion. He didn't see any evidence of God's power in his past life or in his present troubles.

85

He accused God of forgetting him. He said, "Lord, why are You standing aloof and far away? Why do You hide when I need You the most?" (Ps. 10:1)

He later became even more direct: "How long will You forget me, Lord? Forever? How long will You look the other way when I am in need?" (13:1)

What David needed to bring him out of his amnesia was a 29¢ notebook of his prayer requests and their answers.

Today I remembered *my* notebook. I flipped the pages back over two months of requests and answers. Why didn't I do it before? It astounded me. I'd forgotten what God had done. In forgetting how faithful God was to me in the past, I'd left myself wide open to the blows of my new crisis.

Maybe David did have some sort of notebook. I don't know. But something restored his memory, because he returned to his senses and said, "But I will always trust in You and in Your mercy and shall rejoice in Your salvation. I will sing to the Lord because He has blessed me so richly!" (vv. 5-6)

There it is! We know we will have hassles and crises (Jesus told us that), but let's not forget: God can be trusted. He heard us and worked in our lives in the past; He can work now, in the present.

Wow! Look at That!

One of the most precious things my mother developed in me was the sense of wonder.

I guess all children are born with a sense of wonder, but to reach adulthood with it intact and fully matured is practically a miracle.

I was only a second—or third—grader when I first noticed a field of yellow dandelions while on my way home from school one day. I waded into that glorious golden sea of sunshine, picked all the blossoms my hands could hold, and ran all the way home. I flung the door open wide and shouted, "Here, Mother, *these are for you!*"

At that moment, my mother was engaged in a Bible study with a roomful of ladies from our church. She had two options; shush me up, or develop my sense of wonder.

In slow magnificent awe she laid her books on the table, knelt beside me, and took my gift.

"Oh, they are beautiful, beautiful, beautiful," she

said over and over again. (She *could* have told me they were messy weeds.) "I love them because you gave them to me." (She *could* have given me a lecture on picking flowers on private property.) "I'm going to set them on our table for our centerpiece tonight." (She *could* have told me they'd never last the afternoon and aside from drooping would make my father sneeze.)

David, the psalmist, was never too old to be lost in the awe and wonder of really seeing things.

Someone else might have only seen a few straggly old cows here and there, but David wrote about God owning the cattle on a thousand hills (Ps. 50:10). Someone else might have had the same canopy of stars overhead night after night without ever being moved by their majesty, but David wrote:

"The heavens are telling the glory of God; they are a marvelous display of His craftsmanship. Day and night they keep on telling about God" (19:1-2).

Perhaps someone had taken the time to develop the God-given trait of wonder in David, to expand it and encourage it. The world has been richer ever since because of his inspired sense of awe.

Our sense of wonder can open the lenses in our eyes so that when we look at things we *really* see them. I pray God keeps me constantly reminded of my heritage of wonder as I train my own children and myself to *see everything* there is to see.

Spring!

The hills surrounding my home have slipped into their bright green velvet coats as if they are all attending someone's birthday party. Blooming mustard plants splash the green with bursts of yellow paint. Purple spires and yellow daisies proudly proclaim their aliveness. California poppies gently ripple and skip over the hills like orange flames. Our Lord, the master Designer, has exquisite creative ability!

Why all these words on spring? I guess it's just because in the press of life's hectic schedules and crises, in the tense yet boring routine of our work, and in the waiting for prayers to be answered, we all tend to isolate and withdraw into our problems. We block out the great and glorious—yet everyday—wonders God would have us enjoy.

Yesterday a woman complained for 30 minutes about her husband who has been late every evening for dinner during the last month. She's completely lost sight of the fact her husband has a good job, he is healthy, he is home, and he's a marvelous Christian husband and father. The woman missed so much of God's joy around her by dwelling on one inconvenience.

I suspect David was aware of how easy it is to focus on our problems and how difficult it is to lift our sights beyond our circumstances. He asked the Lord specifically to teach him to number his days. As I read his psalms, I see a writer who has indeed tasted from just about every bitter cup known to mankind, yet never lost his sense of wonder.

One of the most devastating symptoms of emotional and spiritual separation in marriages today is the lessening of wonderment about each other. The sense of wonder in marriage enables a husband to say to his wife, "I don't know how you do it, but here we are, after 25 years and you still manage to surprise and delight me."

Today, I've been tempted to succumb to weary discouragement, to sink into feeling *Oh, what's the use?* Yet there are those hills outside!

They shout at me; they yell to me; they almost

dance before me with their message: "It is spring...
God is alive...all is not lost....He cares!"

I hear Him whisper through the green grass and the
fields of flowers. "My child, I am as alive as these hills!
I have risen and I am in complete control. Trust Me,
come to Me, bring Me your burdens, and leave them
with Me. I've come so you'd have abundant life! Look
up to the hills for I will be your strength."

Thank You, Lord, for springtime!

TBC
Syndrome

She dragged herself into choir on Sunday morning.... He asked his wife if they could skip the after church get-together.... They said they'd like to come to the special meetings, but they didn't think they'd be able to make it.

These people all have one thing in common; they are afflicted with the TBC syndrome.

The "Tired Blood Christian" syndrome intrigues me because I am sometimes its victim. I'd been wondering what the contributing factors were when my pastor startled me with this statement one Sunday morning: "Tired Christians are people who continually try to be everything to everybody." He went on to talk about our tiring double approach to life.

If we are with a group from the office and they are not Christians, we try to be one of them so we will not be thought of as odd or different. We want them to accept us. If we are with a group of committed Christians, even our language and tonal qualities take on spiritual overtones. We want them to accept us.

By the end of the week, after shifting gears from one group to another, we find ourselves close to exhaustion from the expended energy we've given to the project of being accepted. We suffer from tired everything.

The Bible warns about being double-minded, but we have such a tremendous need to be accepted we wear ourselves to a frazzle trying to achieve that acceptance.

I've written myself some prescriptions for my TBC syndrome to help me stop wasting tons of energy on being accepted by people. It seems to me that whatever I may accomplish in life depends on exactly what I believe. So I will use my faith, my belief in Christ, and my knowledge that because I am His I have His mind.

Prescription No.1—I will eat well-balanced nutritional foods found in God's Word. (I will do this daily without light snacking or cutting calories.)

Prescription No.2—I will build up my muscles of faith by exercising and maintaining a prayer life. (This is God's tonic.)

Prescription No.3—I will sleep deeply at night, secure in the knowledge that I am not to try to impress or be accepted by people. Of greatest importance is that God knows, forgives, loves, and accepts me.

Prescription No.4—Early every morning I will renew my energy by giving the day "unto Him that is able to do exceeding abundantly above all that we ask or think, according to the power that worketh in us" (Eph. 3:20, KJV).

Holy
or Hectic?

By Saturday afternoon, my inner tension had built
sufficiently for me to stop and ask myself, *What's the
matter?* Then I remembered. *Tomorrow is Sunday!*

How awful! The day that was supposed to mean
tremendous things only meant horrible, hectic hap-
penings to me. I knew the routine well:

Sunday morning—usual headache, grumpy husband.

Sunday noon—arguing children, burned roast.

Sunday afternoon—indigestion.

Sunday night—exhaustion.

I talked to the Lord about our Sundays and asked
Him for a plan. We needed a good plan, one that
would make Sunday a glorious spiritual day for the
whole family. A plan that would help us avoid being
physically and spiritually exhausted on Monday.

The Lord started His plan with me. My usual Sunday morning practice was to stay in bed as long as I
could. Of course, that left everyone else rushed,

disoriented, and without much breakfast. The Lord suggested I get up ahead of everyone else, fix a decent breakfast, and start dinner. (So I didn't care for the plan! I decided I'd better try it anyway.)

The Lord reminded me that, while Satan cannot take away our salvation, he certainly pressures us at our weakest points. My headache, for example, was at its worst just as I was singing in the choir. My husband's stomach growled all through the sermon, making him even more grumpy. The trip home was punctuated by hungry, angry children wrestling in the backseat.

We had a family conference the following Thursday night. I explained Sundays (not that anyone needed it) and ended by telling them we were not going to be robbed of that great day. We talked about what each of us could do to help Sundays get off to the right start.

I promised to get up early, get us a decent breakfast, and start plans for dinner. My husband promised to control his grumpiness. Our children would try to keep from fighting.

Sunday came, and many, many Sundays have followed. Not all have been divinely perfect, but none has been the old Hectic Fever type either.

God healed our Sundays.

I now better appreciate the beautiful beatitude, "Happy are those who strive for peace—they shall be called the sons of God" (Matt. 5:9). When as a family we began to strive for peace, God gave us holy—happy—Sundays.

The
Thankful
List

It's Thanksgiving time again. I know it because everyone is talking about it. My mailman, usually very
quiet, admonished me this morning with, "Count
your blessings." The ad on the billboard by the freeway read, *Put a little thanks into your life,* and a
delivery boy I'd never seen before called cheerily to
me, "Happy Thanksgiving!" So all this has set me to
wondering just what I am thankful for.

If I were to write a list of the things I'm thankful for,
I'd put down all the good things of life, like a loving
marriage, great children, and our growth this year in
the Lord.

But as I look over my list, I wonder about the
difficult things of the year. Should they be on the list
too? Our Lord clearly reveals in His Word that we are
to be thankful and grateful for *all* things.

My list does not include some suffering I had this
year, yet in order for my patience to grow (the Epistle
of James tells us) I need problems, pain, and suffering.

My list includes none of the past months' disappointment, yet it was exactly when my disappointment was greatest that Jesus was especially close and comforting to me. My list makes no mention of the irritating "thorn" in my life, yet that very thorn has made me search out answers in God's Word—and my strength has doubled!

All day I've been singing Audrey Mieir's song "Don't Spare Me":

Don't spare me trouble if it will bring me close to Thee.

Don't spare me heartache, You bore a broken heart for me.

Don't spare me loneliness, for I recall Gethsemane.

Don't spare me anything that You endured for me.

But give me strength to follow Thee. *

This is quite a Thanksgiving song. It is not easy to make out a heartache, pain, and disappointment list and then be thankful over it, yet the Old Testament prophet did such a thing when his list read:

"Even though the fig trees are all destroyed, and there is neither blossom left nor fruit, and though the olive crops all fail, and the fields lie barren; even if the flocks die in the fields and the cattle barns are empty, yet I will rejoice in the Lord; I will be happy in the God of my salvation" (Hab. 3:17-18).

The secret is in the fact that he did not make up his list of praise and thanksgiving by how he *felt* emotionally. He made it a matter of will. He, like the psalmist, says, "I will praise. . . " *That's* thanksgiving!

I'm making out a new list.

"A Whole Man"

Some of the most moving experiences I've ever had have been in connection with the dozen tours I've made for the Chaplain's Division of the U.S. Army. Singing and speaking in open-wound hospital wards has been difficult; yet those performances I cherish the most.

After I finished singing in five wards one day at Camp Zama, Japan, I went back to speak to one more soldier before I left. As I walked to the nearest bed, I noticed the boy had no visible wounds, so I started kidding him about his taking up a bed when others were sick.

He smiled and kidded back, then explained, "Actually, Ma'am, the specialists are upstairs now, and they are deciding whether they will amputate both my legs."

I tried to recover some mental balance and simply responded, "Is that scary?"

"Yes, Ma'am," he said slowly, "it is, especially since I

have an 18-month-old son I've never seen, and when I do see him I don't want to be cut off to half a man—I want to be a *whole* man."

Squeezing his hand, I asked him if I could pray. He said yes and shut his eyes. Then I wondered *what* I would pray.

The Lord reminded me of something my pastor had said not too long before: "Man's greatest problem is his brokenness, and his greatest need is to be made whole."

So I began, "O Lord, all day I've seen and talked with men who have no arms, no legs, and, some, no faces. I'll never forget the horror of it all, but far more tragic is the man whose heart is fragmented."

I continued praying, not for that young man's impending surgery, but for his heart to be made whole by the touch of Jesus so it could hold forgiveness, joy, and the presence of God. When I finished his face was absolutely shining and he yelled, "Wow! How did you know that's what I needed?" Then he excitedly called the chaplain and said, "Go upstairs and tell them I'm ready for their verdict. I don't care what they say—I'm ready. I'm a *whole* man no matter *what.*"

Months later, the hospital chaplain told me they did not amputate and that the soldier had a fantastic witness to the joy of Christ.

Many times since then when I've been all absorbed in what I might lose, what I might not get, or what I might miss, I've remembered that soldier, and the Lord has reminded me that the real issue is my heart's condition, being *whole* inside. And I've thanked the Lord over and over for the lesson I was given that day at Camp Zama Hospital.

For
These
Fragile
Times

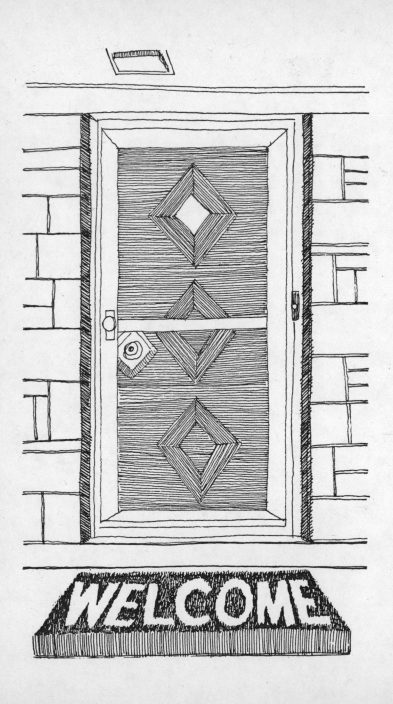

Welcome Or?

All day long I've been smiling over the humorous truth of a cartoon I saw. A little boy and his friend were looking down at the word *Welcome* on the doormat. Pointing to it the boy said, "That's the first thing I learned to read. It says, *'Wipe your feet!'* "

I thought about all the times we've said one thing, but communicated quite another.

Spoken: "Pick up your clothes; your room is a mess!"

Communicated: "You are so dumb! How long am I going to have to tell you these things?"

Spoken: "Hello, how are you?"

Communicated: "I really don't have time to listen or care."

Spoken: "Darling, you do it *this* way."

Communicated: "Stupid!"

Since some claim that only seven percent of what we communicate is verbal, the rest lies in such things as our vocal pitch, inflections, and facial expression.

Once when I was concentrating on peeling potatoes, I suddenly realized that five-year-old Laurie was standing quite close to me, studying me seriously. Looking gravely into my eyes, she said, "Mother, are you happy to see me?"

I bent down, hugged her, and reassured her of my love and realized that she was *reading my face.* I was frowning at those potatoes, and she took it personally.

How many times are we engrossed in our own problematic world to the point that our faces show no love or kindness? There comes a time in all our lives when we *are* held accountable for the expressions on our faces.

When we speak, we very often communicate something quite opposite from our words because we are not being honest. I don't mean we should just say whatever we feel, even if it tears down and destroys. Instead, we should ask God for an honest love for others. Then our kind words will come across that way.

We also need to back up our words with honest, Christlike living, even on Mondays.

Have you ever watched a car with a bumper sticker that reads, *Smile, God loves you,* weave in and out of lanes and cut off other cars? I have, and thought, *I'm smiling because God loves me, but I'm not too sure God is smiling at the driver.* He was not backing up his sticker with honest Christlike driving.

Back to my cartoon—perhaps it would be more honest if most doormats read:

WIPE YOUR FEET—PLEASE?

Trophy Time

We live in an age that delights in giving awards. We have trophies for sports; prizes for literary and journalistic achievement; awards for medicine, science, and the arts.

We even have the man-, woman-, boy-, and girl-of-the-year awards. Nothing gives us more delight than giving awards—except possibly receiving them.

So I've drawn up my own list this year. And I now present the Joyce Landorf Trophies. . . .

To the girl who kept quiet at lunchtime when everyone else was freely giving her their critical opinions about a mutual friend. "A true friend is always loyal" (Prov. 17:17).

To the woman who accepted the nomination to be women's missionary president even though it scares her to death and she knows someone else could do a better job. "Let everyone be sure that he is doing his very best, for then he will have the personal satisfaction of work well done, and won't need to compare himself with someone else" (Gal. 6:4).

To the woman who turned down the same nomination because she felt she'd be spreading herself too thin over God's priorities for her life. "You made my body, Lord; now give me sense to heed Your Laws" (Ps. 119:73).

To the man who illegally cut in front of me on the freeway and then, realizing his mistake, waved an apology. "A man who refuses to admit his mistakes can never be successful. But if he confesses and forsakes them, he gets another chance" (Prov. 28:13).

To the woman who came to visit me while I was still in bed with the flu and didn't ask, "How are you?" but rather, "Which shall I clean first—the kitchen or the bathroom?" "Humility and reverence for the Lord will make you both wise and honored" (Prov. 15:33).

To the person who has just learned he has terminal cancer but says, "I belong to the Lord. He will not take me home to Him one minute sooner or later than He wants to, so I'll just be ready."

"We try to live in such a way that no one will ever be offended or kept back from finding the Lord by the way we act, so that no one can find fault with us and blame it on the Lord. In fact, in everything we do we try to show that we are true ministers of God" (2 Cor. 6:3-4).

Back to the Valley

After a fantastic morning of a spiritual retreat with around a thousand women in Arizona, a young mother of seven children said to me, "I'm so high right now, spiritually, but I've been here before. What happens when I go home is that I come crashing down. How can I avoid the 'back to reality' letdown?"

I was reminded of the disciples who wanted to stay on the mountaintop with the Lord, but He led them gently down off the mountain and back to the valley of the nitty-gritty (Matt. 17).

Why is it so hard to go back down off the mountaintop and pick up living in the valley? Part of the answer lies in the fact that the people in the valley (in your house) have *not* been with you. They have not heard what you have heard and they have not experienced the spiritual awakening or touch that you have had.

You come bursting in the door with all kinds of terrific things to tell about, experiences to share and you find your children have had a field day wrecking your house, your washer broke, the baby-sitter didn't show up, your husband was stuck with the job, and the *very* last thing *anyone* wants to hear is "what a wonderful time you had!"

I remember a teenager who accepted Christ at camp one summer. He could hardly wait to get home to share the news with his parents. He ran into the house not looking where he was going and yelled, "Mom, Dad, guess what—I've become a Christian!"

His mother took one look at him and said, "You just dumped a ton of dirt on my clean floor! Go outside and get cleaned up."

The boy was utterly spun off his mountain. He crashed and bounced on the rocks in the valley below, and he never shared any more of his mountaintop experiences at home because he was so devastated by his mother's remark.

When we go home, finish a book, or try to relate what a speaker has said, we must make it a rule of thumb that when we share, it will not be show-and-tell time.

What it really is, is *show* time. *Without telling, show your family, your mate, and your friends that something has transpired.*

If you *tell* them, you may find they are an unwilling or preoccupied audience. Also, what was funny or deeply moving may lose everything in your translation of it. Then you begin to suffer from the back-to-reality letdown and the snappy little voice of Satan says, "See, you didn't have such a mountaintop experience after all. If you had, it certainly would have lasted longer."

Nonsense! The Lord led His disciples off the

mountain and down into the valley because that's where they *lived.* That valley is the place we really mature, expand, and grow from what we saw and heard up on the mountaintop. The valley of living is where God puts His mountaintop experiences into real practical, everyday, nitty-gritty lessons.

When you get home from a mountaintop experience, walk in the door, thank the husband who babysat, hug the messy children, cook them a good dinner, and just tell them you really love them. Believe me, they'll *know* something's happened and that you've had quite an experience from the glow on your face.

It Comes with a Guarantee

I try to buy brand-name products that come with some sort of guarantee. The durability of an item and the company's backing are very important to me. It doesn't matter if it's a washing machine or a pair of jeans, I want to know the product will hold up.

Once, when we needed a mattress for our son's bed, I did not heed this concept of quality buying. I simply got terribly frustrated one day, stopped changing the sheets on the lumpy old mattress, and went to town. I bought the first mattress in sight.

A few months later it was such a disaster we had to replace it. While my husband has forgiven me for buying it, he's never really truly forgotten it. Mention that mattress to our son and he immediately goes into his "Hunchback of Notre Dame" act.

We replaced the mattress with a good one. It had a higher price tag, but it also had a guarantee.

There isn't much in life that's *really* guaranteed today. Usually it's only for one year or 12,000 miles, whichever comes first. Yet I want the best for my money, and I like the manufacturer to possess an old-fashioned thing called "pride in workmanship."

The Bible states clearly that God believes in giving guarantees and standing behind His contractual promises. A durable, secure guarantee is written out in no uncertain terms in Revelation 2:10.

The guarantee covers the times in our lives when (for various reasons) we must suffer. God does not make the false claim that He will *remove* the suffering. Rather: "Be thou faithful unto death, and I will give thee a crown of life" (KJV).

It's just like me to run impulsively out, grab at straws, and buy some quick easy line of thought—only to find I'm the loser.

The Bible offers another sure guarantee in Deuteronomy 31:6. "The Lord thy God, He it is that doth go with thee; He will not fail thee, nor forsake thee" (KJV).

The guarantee works if I (1) remember to do the right thing, and (2) trust myself to the God who made me.

Sometimes suffering, like the old mattress, is so frustrating we forget what God wants us to do, lose sight of what God can do through us, and ignore all the fine print in God's guarantee. But He promises us enduring strength through suffering in a personal contract with One who will never fail us.

I've learned my lesson in the mattress department. I pray I'll remember to read the fine print of God's guarantees, then act in the light of such clear-cut promises.

Fed Up with Christians?

I can't recall all of the story, but it seems that two lions were talking under the Roman Colosseum during the first century. Finally, one lion said to the other lion, "Aren't you just *fed up* with Christians?"

That punchline repeatedly came into focus recently in my mail and in my phone calls and personal encounters. Just this month I've seen, observed, and heard an unnerving number of Christians who say they are "fed up" with other Christians.

It's true that some Christians may seem to be one disappointment to us after another. They can be dishonest, disloyal, and even disagreeable. We may not even understand another's doctrine or theology.

But I'm not writing this to discuss how Christians have disappointed us. Rather, I want to point out at least three consequences of becoming "fed up" with other Christians.

First, we become limited persons. When we spend time judging the disappointing lives of other Christians, we are robbed of valuable time to concentrate on what God wants to do in *our* lives. The Pharisee who thanked God he wasn't like that "sinner" over there lost his potential for being the man God wanted him to be (Luke 18:11).

The act of focusing on the "failures" of other people limits what God wants to accomplish in *our* lives.

Next, we lose our joy. When we have just *had it* with Christians, we find ourselves in direct disobedience to one of Jesus' most important commands—to love one another (John 15:12). If we say we love Him yet hate our brother and sister, we are liars (1 John 4:20). So, our joy gets very troubled or we lose it altogether. When our joy in Christ is gone, a vacancy is left in our souls. Soon moodiness and depression move in.

Finally, Satan has a good laugh. When we spend time commiserating with friends about how Christians have let us down, the background music we hear is Satan chuckling. He knows he can't erase our names from God's Book of Life, but he *can* keep our eyes on the failures of other Christians—and cause us to lose our joy.

If you've reached the *I'm-fed-up-with-Christians* stage, I pray God will restore to you *His* marvelous, luminous joy, and show you your own priceless potential in Him.

That's what He had to do with *me* today.

Mad As a Wet Hen

Experts tell us that anger, a difficult-to-deal-with emotion, is triggered by four main causes:

1. Extreme fatigue—such as what a young mother with two children under four years of age experiences.

2. Extreme embarrassment—especially in front of friends, family, or in full view of strangers.

3. Extreme rejection—such as one parent (or both) never giving their child approval.

4. Extreme frustration—such as doing the very best job and then seeing everything go wrong.

Some seem to think that, as Christians, we should not show anger. I don't think that's true. Anger is a God-given emotion. It's how a Christian handles and controls anger that either causes or keeps him from sin.

We are told in the Book of Galatians that the fruit of the Spirit is love, joy, peace, self-control. ... But, mind you, we must be walking in the Spirit in order for these fruit to be produced in our lives.

That brings me to the word *control.* We can control our anger, temper, and thoughts if we want to. It may mean getting up each day and deciding who's going to be in control of our life.

We can let Satan be in charge and watch everything fall apart, or we can let the Holy Spirit be in charge and experience the fruit of His power.

Our emotional reactions can hurt others if the Spirit isn't in control. So when we first feel the surge of anger, we need to:

1. Recognize what problem has brought the anger into focus (fatigue, embarrassment, rejection, or frustration).

2. Ask for the Holy Spirit's control in handling it. The Bible says, "Be ye angry, and sin not" (Eph. 4:26, KJV). So evidently the emotion of anger in itself is not a sin. But to harm someone verbally, emotionally, or physically is.

I know that I will grow angry from time to time, but if I'm walking in the Spirit, He will give me the power to control the by-product of my emotional reaction.

One other word about anger. Since the emotion of anger causes many biochemical reactions, such as the rise of blood pressure, we need to channel the added pressure off in some way.

I've found that vacuuming every rug in the house releases much of my tension. And it gets rather funny when my daughter walks in, sees the clean carpets, and asks, "Who were you mad at today?"

Everything Up-to-Date

Just three weeks ago today, as I write this, my lovely mother-in-law, Margaret Landorf, died. She was 69 years old. My father-in-law is 75 and retired. They became Christians years ago and were joyfully serving the Lord in their little retirement community.

On the morning of her death, Mom and Dad Landorf had breakfast together and, as usual, finished by having devotions. They were into 2 Corinthians. After praying together, they did some yard work. Mom watered her flowers, cut fresh rhubarb from her garden, and finished the morning in the kitchen.

While Mom was working on the first square of an afghan she was making for our daughter, she said she was sleepy. As she was taking a nap in the bedroom, Dad watched a game on TV and then he too fell asleep.

A little later in the afternoon, he awoke and went in to awaken Margaret. But she had left him as they slept.

None of us, especially my father-in-law, has quite adjusted to the abruptness of her death.

In time, we will be grateful that her passing was not preceded by a long, debilitating illness, nor heavy medical expenses; but for now we grieve with a keen sense of loss. We know she is with the Lord, and that's a source of comfort, but somehow it is still shocking that we cannot phone her or see her again.

Since I have lost a loved one before, I'm well aware of this grieving process—and of the strong comfort our God has for us in times of loss. I also know how God can use good memories in our healing.

As I think back on her last moments here, I am warmed by the memory of this couple's routine day. There they were, unaware they had only those few hours left together, yet they lived out those hours with everything up-to-date. Two senior citizens with their love of God and each other up-to-date and beautiful. Two children of God with their forgiveness, their joy, and their usefulness all up-to-date and ready to go on a moment's notice.

They had no regrets and no thoughts of *I wish I hadn't said that!* or, *If only I'd done such and such!* They had lived their last morning in God's fullness, love, and grace. Then, when it was time for one of them to go, she went with everything in readiness and all the areas of her life up-to-date. While we are not able yet to look at her things without tears flooding our eyes, we must admit she left under the best of circumstances.

What a way to go! It's the way I pray I'll leave someday—with everything up-to-date and ready.

Do It
Now

We need to make time for three things. (I say *make* time, because we will never *find* the time.)

1. *We need to make time for God.*

Most of us will agree with the truth of that statement, but few of us really carry it out daily. A lazy piano student who won't practice daily never learns the joy of making beautiful music.

Making time for God gives God the opportunity, by our conversing daily with Him and permitting Him to speak to us, to develop all sorts of talents in us.

2. *We need to make time for ourselves.*

I remember a Sunday School class called the J-O-Y class. The initials stood for Jesus first, Others second and Yourselves last. A beautiful goal. But sometimes in our busyness, we put ourselves so far down the list we can't experience real joy.

We need to read a book, take a walk, plant a bush or flower bed, take a class in sewing, or just "sit a spell." We need to take time to reflect on life.

3. *We need to make time for our God-given responsibilities.*

Whatever field of endeavor is ours, we must give it our best. Whether we are in business, at home raising a family, or both, we need to seek God's wisdom in carrying out the highly original plan He has for us.

Put your hand to the plow, the pen, the diaper wash, or the vacuum cleaner and do it without wasting precious moments.

Don't let your worries about the past, present, or future keep you from scheduling these three important segments of time.

Put your yesterdays where they belong—in the past. Release yourself from time's mortgaging grip. The trouble, pain, and sorrow of yesterday is over. It's too late to change it.

God has forgiven all your yesterdays if you trust in Christ. "When sins have once been forever forgiven and forgotten, there is no need to offer more sacrifices to get rid of them" (Heb. 10:18).

Live today enthusiastically, for it will expand your powers of appreciation. We need to count our blessings each morning, then repeat, "This is the day which the Lord hath made; we will rejoice and be glad in it" (Ps. 118:24, KJV).

Welcome tomorrow with no nagging doubts as to its outcome. Remember, one morning the clouds will break open and Jesus will come back and we will be forever with Him!

Who Is RuPaul?

by Nico Medina

illustrated by Andrew Thomson

Penguin Workshop

To all the legendary children—NM

For Rhia and Cerys—AT

PENGUIN WORKSHOP
An Imprint of Penguin Random House LLC, New York

Copyright © 2021 by Penguin Random House LLC. All rights reserved.
Published by Penguin Workshop, an imprint of Penguin Random House LLC, New York.
PENGUIN and PENGUIN WORKSHOP are trademarks of Penguin Books Ltd.
WHO HQ & Design is a registered trademark of Penguin Random House LLC.
Printed in the USA.

Visit us online at www.penguinrandomhouse.com.

Library of Congress Cataloging-in-Publication Data is available upon request.

ISBN 9780593222690 (paperback)   10 9 8 7 6 5 4 3 2 1
ISBN 9780593222706 (library binding)   10 9 8 7 6 5 4 3 2 1

Contents

Who Is RuPaul?

On September 18, 2016, RuPaul made television history. (Or "*her*story," as Ru would say.)

A drag queen—most commonly, a man who dresses up and performs as a woman—had never won an Emmy until then. (Emmys are awards for excellence in TV programming, as chosen by the Television Academy.)

Backstage, RuPaul held back tears as he spoke about "all the kids who watch the show." How it had helped them to "navigate their lives."

The show he was talking about was *RuPaul's Drag Race*. Ru is both the host and judge of the reality-competition show of drag queens from across the United States. The queens all share a passion for performing in drag and compete against one another for a cash prize and the title of America's Next Drag Superstar.

According to Ru, drag isn't something unusual to be feared or looked down upon. "Everybody within the sound of my voice is in drag, right now, whether [they] know it or not," RuPaul has said.

What Ru means is, when anyone puts on clothing, they are getting into some form of costume—some type of "drag." When you go to school, you don't put on your bathing suit. Maybe you put on a uniform. You wear what is expected for a student to wear. People dress in "drag" to go to work. To weddings. Out to dinner.

RuPaul says, "We're all born naked and the rest is drag." What Ru means is that we're all the same—and life is a performance.

By the time *RuPaul's Drag Race* won its first Emmy for Outstanding Reality-Competition Program in 2018, 140 drag queens had competed on the show. Many have gone on to have successful careers and thousands of fans of their own.

"We celebrate people who dance outside the box," RuPaul said after the win. Their "stories need to be told, and I think there is value in those stories for everyone, not just drag queens."

RuPaul had traveled a long road to get to that moment. More than thirty-five years before, he had put on his first wig. It had been over twenty-five years since Ru's song "Supermodel (You Better Work)" had hit the airwaves and made him the world's most famous drag queen. And it was nine years since *Drag Race*'s television debut.

But RuPaul had always known he would be famous. Ru has said that to become a star, you need to *believe* you're a star—and eventually, other people will start believing it, too.

As a child in the 1960s, RuPaul hadn't seen many people like him—people who were gay, even people who were Black—on popular TV shows. But things had changed for the better, and Ru had been a part of that change.

"I have always been a creative person," Ru said. "I've always been able to see different colors that other people were ignoring."

How had RuPaul, who came from very humble beginnings, become such a superstar?

This is his—and *her*—story.

He, She, or They? Drag Is for Everyone

RuPaul was once asked if he wished he'd been born a woman. No, Ru answered, he was happy to be a man. (It is a common misunderstanding that drag queens are men who wish to be women.) When RuPaul dresses in drag, he is performing a character. Ru once joked, "You can call me he, you can call me she . . . as long as you call me."

Some drag queens, however, are transgender or nonbinary. For trans people, their gender (how they feel on the inside) is different from the sex (male or female) they were assigned at birth. Nonbinary people do not identify as entirely male or entirely female. These queens might prefer to be called "she" or "they" (rather than "he") when not performing in drag.

Drag *kings* are people—usually women—who dress and perform as men. Women can be drag *queens*, too. Drag is for anyone who wants to express themselves through a character.

CHAPTER 1
"I Accept My Destiny!"

RuPaul's full name is RuPaul Andre Charles. His mother, Ernestine "Toni" Charles, knew this was an unusual name. Before RuPaul was even born, a fortune-teller had told Toni that her son would be famous. So she named him RuPaul because, she said, "ain't another . . . with a name like that."

Toni and RuPaul's father, Irving, were both

from Louisiana. They had met on a blind date. Soon after, they moved to Houston, Texas, and got married. Ru's older twin sisters, Renae and Renetta, were born in 1953.

Irving Charles had served in the army and fought in the Korean War. After the army, Irving moved the family out west to San Diego, California, where he worked as an electrician. The Charles family moved into a three-bedroom house. Irving built a patio out back.

RuPaul was born on November 17, 1960. His younger sister, Rozy, was born two years later.

Renae, Renetta, Rozy, and RuPaul

Ru Stew

According to RuPaul, the *Ru* in his name comes from the word *roux* (say: ROO). Roux is a mixture of flour and butter that is cooked together and used to thicken soups and stews. A roux is used to make gumbo, a hearty Creole dish of sausage, shrimp, other meats, and vegetables.

RuPaul's mother was Creole. Creole people are of mixed descent: Black (African and Caribbean), European (mostly French and Spanish), and sometimes Native American. Creoles have lived in Louisiana since long before it became part of the United States in 1803.

Life in the Charles house was not always easy. RuPaul's parents fought and yelled a lot. When RuPaul was seven, his parents divorced. His mother became so upset that one day, she didn't get out of bed. That's when Ru's older sisters, Renae and Renetta, became the grown-ups in the house. They took care of Ru and Rozy while Toni got the help she needed.

Eventually, Toni got better and found a good, steady job. She worked at a clinic, then later at a local college.

Young RuPaul always knew that he was different from most boys his age. He was quiet and sensitive. He also loved the cigar commercials on television that featured glamorous women, in sparkling evening gowns, performing to Broadway-style music.

When he was four, RuPaul saw something on television that changed his life forever. Diana Ross and the Supremes, a popular musical group at the time, appeared on *The Ed Sullivan Show* and performed their hit song "Baby Love." Ru was captivated.

For one thing, seeing three Black women on a program like Ed Sullivan's was unusual in the early 1960s. And RuPaul saw himself in Diana Ross, the dazzling lead singer, with her perfect hair, beautiful dress, and big, bright

Diana Ross

smile. He remembers thinking: "That one there, the one in the middle—that's me." He knew then that he wanted to be famous—the center of attention—just like Diana.

RuPaul preferred to be around girls rather than boys. He thought that girls and women expressed their emotions and feelings more than boys did. And he liked to play dress-up in their clothes.

"You should have been a girl, and your sister Rozy should have been a boy," some bullies said to him. The hurtful comments sometimes made RuPaul cry.

Still, RuPaul always did what made him happy: He entertained.

Ru's mom and sisters were his first audience. "Do your thing," Toni would tell him, and Ru would stand up, sing, and dance just like the big stars of the day—people like Tina Turner, Cher, and Elvis Presley.

RuPaul looked up to his mom. He loved her simple yet elegant style. And even though Toni could be tough, she also had a sweet and sensitive side. She had "the strength of a man and the heart of a woman."

RuPaul was not afraid to be himself and look different from everybody else. When he was ten, he bleached and braided his hair. At one point, he had a red Afro seventeen inches deep!

RuPaul and Rozy

Ru attended Alonzo E. Horton Elementary School, just a block from his house, from kindergarten through sixth grade. In seventh grade, he took acting lessons at the local children's theater. Ru loved it so much, he signed up for drama at his new middle school.

But aside from drama classes, Ru was not the best student. He often got caught staring out the classroom windows, daydreaming.

RuPaul would rather be home, reading his magazines about Hollywood movie stars, New York City celebrities, and Motown musicians like the Supremes. He loved everything about pop culture: the cool fashion, movies, music, and art that was popular at that time.

Ru sometimes tagged along with his older sisters when they visited their friends Aletha and Deborah. Their mom worked as a maid on the other side of town, so the kids would have the house to themselves in the afternoons. They could listen to records—and sing and dance—as loud as they wanted to!

By the time he entered high school, tall, thin, and freckly RuPaul really stood out from the crowd. With his soft facial features, he was sometimes mistaken for a girl.

In the mornings before class, RuPaul attended Breakfast Club at the cafeteria. Doughnuts, chips, and chocolate milk were served, and the tables and chairs were pushed aside to make room for the students to dance.

RuPaul remembers one morning watching
from the sidelines as everyone did a dance
called the Bump. Then one day, he and his
friend Michelle showed off a move *no one* at
Breakfast Club had seen before. It was called
the Crypt Walk, the latest dance craze from Los
Angeles. (Ru had seen Olivia Newton-John,
one of his favorite singer-actresses, perform it
on TV.)

Soon everyone was doing the Crypt Walk! That school year, Ru was voted Best Dancer and Best Afro by his ninth-grade classmates. Thinking back on that day, Ru later said that was his way of saying to the universe, "I accept my destiny!" He was born to entertain.

"I accept my destiny!"

What did RuPaul do after introducing the
Crypt Walk to his classmates? Well . . . he did
not go to class. In fact, RuPaul skipped so many
classes, he was expelled.

What would he do now? The family decided it
was best for Ru to move in with his sister Renetta
and her husband, Laurence.

Laurence and Renetta

Laurence was a serious young man with dreams
of his own. He was a good role model for RuPaul.
He'd earned a scholarship to the University of

California, San Diego, and he dreamed big. Laurence loved to drive around La Jolla (say: la HOY-ah), a wealthy neighborhood on the coast, and look at all the big houses. Sometimes he and Renetta brought her family along.

RuPaul liked Laurence. He was the big brother Ru never had. A father figure, even. But just six months after RuPaul moved in with Renetta and Laurence, the couple decided to move two thousand miles away, to Atlanta, Georgia. There were more opportunities there, Laurence said.

Would Ru like to join them?

"Sure," he said, "why not?"

CHAPTER 2
"RuPaul Is Everything"

In the summer of 1976, fifteen-year-old RuPaul arrived in Atlanta. He enrolled at the Northside School of Performing Arts, eager to start acting again.

Ru's drama teacher, Bill Pannell, taught him

and his classmates about method acting—how to become a character from the inside out. Mr. Pannell was passionate, and even though he expected a lot from his students, he once told RuPaul, "Don't take life too seriously."

Ru said this was some of the best advice he had ever received. Whatever problems he might have, life was a gift to be enjoyed. Other people's problems might be much worse than your own.

One problem RuPaul did *not* have was getting noticed! The funky new kid from California developed a reputation for his bright, bold outfits. Ru used Renetta's sewing machine to make his own clothes.

Stripes? Plaid? A cowboy hat? Why not all three?!

Ru still had problems, however, with school. He continued to skip class, and when he did attend, he was often late. After failing his sophomore year, Ru switched schools. But he never graduated.

RuPaul went to work for Laurence, who had started a business buying luxury cars from around the country and selling them in Atlanta.

After Laurence made a sale over the phone, RuPaul would fly to wherever the car was and drive it back to Atlanta. Ru said he must have driven across the country more than a hundred times. He listened to the radio and sang the whole time.

In 1978, Ru attended his first drag show in Atlanta at a club called Numbers. Drag shows feature drag queens telling jokes, dancing, and performing popular songs, either by singing them or by lip-synching (say: SINK-ing), mouthing the words to a song but not singing them aloud.

RuPaul remembers seeing a drag queen lip-synch a disco hit called "Bad Girls" by Donna Summer. The performance was so good, Ru thought he was watching the real Donna Summer onstage!

RuPaul was hooked. He went back to as many drag shows as he could.

In 1981, RuPaul saw a local TV program called *The American Music Show*. It featured a cast of wacky characters with a weird sense of humor that RuPaul could relate to. Ru wrote a letter to the host, Dick Richards, asking if he could come on the show. Lucky for Ru, Dick said yes!

Dick Richards and RuPaul

House and Ball Culture

The drag queen RuPaul saw that night at Numbers was Crystal LaBeija (say: la-BAY-zhuh), from New York City.

Crystal LaBeija

Like many Black and brown gay teenagers, Crystal had been rejected by her family. So in 1977, she founded the House of LaBeija, opening her home as a place where people like her could live together as their own "chosen" and supportive family. Other drag "houses" followed.

Houses competed as teams against rival houses at drag balls, events that were held mainly in the Black neighborhood of Harlem. Drag balls had taken place in Harlem as early as the 1860s and well into the 1920s, continuing for decades. But the scene grew significantly during the 1980s. The beauty and drama of Harlem's ball and house culture was captured in 1990 by the documentary film *Paris Is Burning* and later in the TV drama *Pose.*

RuPaul says that letter was the true beginning of his career in showbiz.

Before his appearance, RuPaul was helping two girlfriends move into a new apartment. He drove the U-Haul moving truck. Struck by inspiration, Ru told his friends they should start a dance group called RuPaul and the U-Hauls and that they should join him on *The American Music Show*. And so they did!

In January 1982, RuPaul and the U-Hauls made their Atlanta television debut. RuPaul made all their costumes, and they performed a dance routine to the song "Shotgun" by Junior Walker & the All Stars. RuPaul *felt* like a star that day.

Ru and the U-Hauls went on to appear regularly on *The American Music Show*. Dick Richards created a new show called *Dancerama USA* that featured a segment called "Learn a Dance with RuPaul."

RuPaul and the U-Hauls

RuPaul was becoming well-known around the Atlanta music scene. He began performing with other acts. It was at one of these shows that RuPaul dressed in drag for the first time.

A local group called the Now Explosion sometimes acted out a wedding during their performances. At these pretend ceremonies, the boys in the band dressed as bridesmaids, and the girls wore tuxedoes. RuPaul joined them for one of these "weddings."

"It was the first time I did real drag in a dress, heels, and with hair," Ru said. He had never even put on a wig before! "The impact it had on people was amazing."

It made RuPaul *feel* amazing, too. RuPaul wanted everyone to know just how much of a star

he was. So he made posters of himself with phrases like "RuPaul Is Everything" and "RuPaul Is Red Hot." He put up hundreds of copies all over town.

At this time, RuPaul began performing in drag more often. But besides the Now Explosion "wedding," he rarely dressed like a woman in the traditional sense. He wore smeared lipstick, messy wigs, ripped T-shirts, and combat boots—sometimes even tall wading boots like fishermen wore!

"It had nothing to do with being gay" or with "wanting to be a woman," RuPaul said. It was about challenging how people thought about the world. He wanted people to look at things in a different way when they watched him perform.

RuPaul moved into his own apartment. After

RuPaul and the U-Hauls broke up, Ru formed a punk-rock group with two other friends. They performed around Atlanta and up and down the East Coast—they even played in New York City!

RuPaul in New York City

The band broke up in 1984. That year, RuPaul met a local drag queen named Bunny while dancing backup for the Now Explosion. They became fast friends and shopped together at local thrift stores, looking for cheap used clothes to turn into wild outfits.

They didn't want sparkly evening gowns or "any of that polish," Bunny said. They were both rock-and-roll queens. "We . . . broke all the rules," RuPaul said.

Ru continued to host events and put on shows around Atlanta. He sold short books he had written and postcards to anyone who would buy them. Some nights, he sold every copy he had!

Ru, Bunny, and their friends also made campy home movies and sold copies of them around town. (People use the word *camp* to mean something that is done in an exaggerated, theatrical, and often silly style.)

But RuPaul knew he was destined for bigger things.

He remembered being twelve years old back in San Diego, reading issue after issue of Andy Warhol's *Interview* magazine. Ru had learned that to make it big, he would first have to become a downtown New York celebrity.

CHAPTER 3
Ups and Downs

In the summer of 1984, RuPaul put together a show called *RuPaul Is Red Hot!* Bunny and a few other Atlanta drag queens joined as costars. They traveled to New York City to perform Ru's show at the Pyramid Club in the city's East Village neighborhood.

Andy Warhol (1928–1987)

Andy Warhol once said, "In the future, everyone will be world-famous for fifteen minutes."

Andy was born in Pittsburgh, Pennsylvania. At eight years old, he contracted a rare disease that confined him to his bed for months. During his illness, Andy's mother gave him his first drawing lessons. Andy moved to New York City in 1949, where he worked as a commercial artist for clients like *Glamour* and *Vogue* magazines before focusing on his own artwork.

In 1962, he painted one of his most famous works, *Campbell's Soup Cans*. This was the beginning of the "pop" ("popular") art movement, which turned everyday elements of people's lives—things like Coke bottles and hamburgers—into art. Warhol also painted a series of celebrity portraits in the same bold, bright style, including one of the actress Marilyn Monroe. He quickly became a celebrity himself, and his art studio—called the Factory—became a popular hangout for artists, musicians, and fashionable New Yorkers. In 1969, he founded *Interview* magazine, which publishes new issues to this day.

After the run of shows ended, Ru and his friends decided to stay in New York. They met an old friend of Dick Richards's from back in Atlanta named Nelson, who showed them around the city. Nelson introduced them to the work of the creative queer people who had come before them—like playwright Tennessee Williams and author Truman Capote.

Nelson always carried a video camera, and RuPaul was always happy to put on a performance. In one video, RuPaul tells the camera, "I'm gonna take off like a stick of dynamite."

But life in New York wasn't easy. Ru and Bunny made forty dollars a night dancing at the Pyramid Club, but Ru didn't have a place to live. Some nights, he stayed with Nelson or other friends.

Other nights, he and Floydd—another friend from Atlanta—would stay out all night, then sleep in parks during the day. Come Christmastime, Floydd and Ru decided to return home.

Bunny stayed in New York, changed her name to the "Lady" Bunny, and founded Wigstock in 1984. This drag-queen performance festival soon grew to attract thousands of people every year.

In 1985, RuPaul began to rethink his act in Atlanta. Dick Richards offered him a record deal. Ru starred in local theater productions and more than a dozen movies. He sold video cassettes of the films out of shopping carts at local bars and clubs.

One of Ru's movie characters, a fashion model who was also an undercover spy named Starrbooty, starred in three movies. Ru, with his massive Mohawk and creative, self-designed looks, gave each performance his signature, over-the-top best. And it was always in his contract that RuPaul's name appeared above the movie title. After all, he was the star!

Ru also worked at a local gay bar called Weekends. When the bar owners reopened the old movie theater next door, RuPaul began to emcee, or host, drag pageants and lip-synching competitions there. He watched videos of himself onstage to improve his skills as an entertainer. Ru called his time at Weekends his "college years."

By 1987, Ru had really made a name for himself in Atlanta. But he was growing restless.

It was time to give New York another try.

That summer, he and a couple of friends—DJ Larry Tee and another Atlanta drag queen called Lahoma—piled into a van to make the journey. On the drive, one of the back tires blew out, and the van flipped over. Their belongings scattered across the highway.

No one was hurt, but this felt like a sign of things to come.

Finding success in New York City was no easier the second time around for RuPaul. By the spring of 1988, he was back in Atlanta. Although Ru returned to New York again that summer, things were just not happening the way he had hoped.

Ru tried his luck in Los Angeles next, moving in with his younger sister, Rozy. But he couldn't find work, and Rozy gave him until November 17, his twenty-eighth birthday, to find a new place to live. It was a dark and difficult time. Ru went to San Diego to spend the holidays with his mother. But where would he go from there?

First, he rested. He quit smoking and grew a beard. He spent time getting to know his eleven-year-old niece Morgan. He ate well, and he relaxed.

Ru also talked on the phone with DJ Larry Tee who, after more than a year in New York, had found success in the nightclub scene. Larry told

RuPaul that he was a star and that Ru should come back. He offered to help Ru out when he arrived.

So in the new year, RuPaul returned to New York City yet again.

But this time would be different.

Larry Tee

CHAPTER 4
Queen of Manhattan

In the New York nightclub scene in 1989, the trendy "look" for drag queens was "realness." That meant that queens looked less camp and more like "real" women.

So RuPaul reinvented himself.

He traded in his Mohawk for a big blond wig. He shaved his legs. And no more ripped T-shirts and wading boots. When RuPaul walked into a club, he wanted to be the most glamorous, gorgeous woman in the room!

The late 1980s and early 1990s marked the era of the Club Kids. The Club Kids were party promoters whose job was to bring crowds into nightclubs. Before going out on the town, the Club Kids would dress up in outrageous, imaginative, and attention-grabbing looks. They used their creativity to turn these parties into must-see events that no one wanted to miss.

"A Club Kid was a little crazier than a drag queen," Lady Bunny said. They might "dress up as an alien or a dog bowl . . . from the waist up, and a policeman from the waist down."

But Club Kids were about more than dressing up. RuPaul said they were about "people being free spirits." Club Kid culture would go on to inspire the drag, art, and fashion worlds for years beyond the 1990s.

While RuPaul didn't dress like the Club Kids, he became just as well-known in New York City nightclubs. At seven feet tall in heels and hair, he was hard to miss!

Susanne Bartsch

Susanne Bartsch—who became "the Mother of all Club Kids" and continues to throw parties today—hired Ru to dance at some of her legendary events.

RuPaul gave it his all, every single time. He didn't just dance—he *performed*! RuPaul was a show all by himself.

Susanne clearly respected Ru's talent. She told him that he had what it took to become a true pop star.

The summer after Ru returned to New York, Larry Tee started throwing a new party called the Love Machine. Larry paid RuPaul a hundred dollars a week to host shows, lip-synch, and dance there.

"Everybody say love!" Ru would call out to the partygoers.

"Love!" everyone would shout back.

Lady Bunny, Floydd, and Lahoma—all of Ru's Atlanta friends—made the Love Machine their home base. Their easy Southern charm took New York by storm, and the Love Machine quickly became the hottest party in town.

Tools of the Trade

A drag queen's character is typically an exaggerated, campy image of how women look. To create this illusion, drag queens have some tricks up their sleeves:

Makeup—Drag queens paint their faces "for the back row," meaning someone watching a drag show from the back of the crowd can still see a drag queen's expressive face in great detail.

Hair—Sometimes, one wig is not enough! Queens sometimes "stack" multiple wigs together to create a big, attention-grabbing shape.

Corset—Tight-fitting garment that goes above the hips and under the chest, to give the illusion of a small waist.

Padding—Gives a drag queen wider hips.

Around this time, the B-52's—a pop-music group from back home in Georgia— asked RuPaul to appear in a music video for their hit song "Love Shack." Ru showed up to the video shoot in an all-white two-piece jumpsuit, bright gold jewelry, and a large Afro wig. He brought his dance-party energy to the set!

By January 1990, a year after moving back to New York, RuPaul was becoming very well-known. A group of downtown club owners and party promoters named him "Queen of Manhattan." This was a big deal in the New York nightlife community, and Ru was the first Black person to earn the title.

At last, RuPaul had arrived!

But with success came pressure. RuPaul was living a fast-paced life, and for years, he had turned to drugs and alcohol during his long, party-filled nights.

So as his reign as Queen of Manhattan came to a close at the end of 1990, RuPaul decided to quit his bad habits—and reinvent himself once again.

CHAPTER 5
Supermodel of the World

In 1991, RuPaul joined World of Wonder, a production company founded by Randy Barbato and Fenton Bailey. Randy and Fenton had met RuPaul in New York in the early 1980s and had produced his *Starrbooty* album. Now they became Ru's managers. Soon, Ru had a contract with Tommy Boy Records.

RuPaul got busy writing new music. He was also promoting "I Got That Feeling," a new song he and Larry Tee had written the year before. But when Ru performed "Feeling" for audiences, he didn't appear in his signature, glamorous drag-queen look.

RuPaul didn't think the world beyond the New York City club scene was ready for a drag queen to be a pop star. But people kept asking what had happened to his Starrbooty character. RuPaul began to realize that fans really wanted to see him perform in drag.

Ru had never imagined he would become famous by performing in drag, but he decided to go all out. If this was what his fans wanted, he would give them "the longest legs, the highest shoes," and "the biggest hair" he could!

He would give them a Supermodel of the World.

In the early 1990s, fashion models like Naomi Campbell, Linda Evangelista, Claudia Schiffer, and Christy Turlington were major international celebrities. These "supermodels" posed in exotic

locations around the world for stylish fashion shoots. They earned large salaries and were photographed wherever they went.

RuPaul's newest song, "Supermodel (You Better Work)," captured the excitement of the moment. Ru premiered it with a live performance at Lady Bunny's Wigstock festival on Labor Day 1992. The single was released on Ru's birthay in November of that year. A full album, *Supermodel of the World*, followed in 1993.

In the "Supermodel" music video, RuPaul plays a model on a photo shoot in New York City. She strikes poses for the camera. She splashes around in a fountain in front of the famous Plaza Hotel. She struts down the sidewalk with a group of schoolgirls like they are walking a fashion-show runway.

Perhaps remembering his drama teacher Mr. Pannell's advice, RuPaul also had fun in the video, not taking herself *too* seriously. As she lip-synched

to the catchy lyrics, she made silly, exaggerated faces for the camera.

"Supermodel" became a hit, reaching number two on the dance charts. MTV, a cable network that showed music videos, aired the video over and over again. Most people around the country had never seen a drag queen before, in person *or* on television. But there was RuPaul, front and center: seven feet of legs, heels, hair, and attitude.

RuPaul appeared on *The Arsenio Hall Show*,

a popular late-night talk show. Backstage, he was nervous. But then Ru remembered all the years of practice he'd had performing for the camera, entertaining audiences, and making people feel good.

After performing "Supermodel," Ru sat down to chat with Arsenio and the studio audience. Ru had everyone laughing, but he also delivered a serious, heartfelt message. "Everybody is really

the same," RuPaul said. "Everybody wants to be loved" and "should be respected." That love, he said, started with loving yourself.

Ru said he was lucky his family accepted him for who he was, because there were many other gay people—children and adults—who couldn't say the same. He hoped that by appearing on a program like Arsenio's, he might inspire people watching at home, the same way that seeing a young Black woman like Diana Ross on *The Ed Sullivan Show* had inspired him.

"Everybody say love!" he called to the crowd.

"Love!" they responded.

America was only just meeting RuPaul, but RuPaul had worked his whole life for this moment. He was no newcomer. From rowdy Atlanta bars to smoky New York City nightclubs, he had put in the time and effort.

Just like Ru's song says, if you want to be a superstar: "You better *work*."

A Brief History of Drag

Dressing in the traditional clothing of the opposite sex—called cross-dressing—has existed throughout history. Ancient civilizations from the Egyptians to the Aztecs incorporated cross-dressing into religious ceremonies. During William Shakespeare's time, women's roles onstage were played by men. The word *drag* may have originated in the 1800s theater scene because the men's dresses would "drag" on the floor. In the early 1900s, female impersonation—men performing as women—became popularized in live vaudeville acts, which combined music, dance, and comedy. Female impersonation by non-queer men continued in movies like *Some Like It Hot* (1959) and *Mrs. Doubtfire* (1993). Drag became more closely connected with gay culture during Prohibition in the 1920s, when liquor was outlawed in the United

States, and queer people—including drag queens—met in secret, illegal bars called speakeasies. Drag continued to evolve in local gay bars, before going nationwide in 1972 with the first Miss Gay America pageant.

Men in drag in the late 1800s

CHAPTER 6
"Windows of Opportunity"

In Atlanta, RuPaul Was Everything. At the Pyramid Club, RuPaul Was Red Hot. And now . . . RuPaul Was *Everywhere*!

The song "Supermodel" played at New York Fashion Week runway shows. It was used in a commercial for Duracell batteries. RuPaul performed it at the Cannes Film Festival in France. He presented at the MTV Video Music Awards. And Ru's yearlong concert tour played to packed crowds across the United States and Europe.

A few years earlier, after RuPaul had moved back in with his mom in San Diego, Toni told her son, "Everything will change, so pay it no mind." She sure was right. What a difference five years had made!

The world had changed a lot in that time, too. Queer people everywhere—people who were gay, lesbian, bisexual, and transgender—were "coming out of the closet." They were declaring to friends, family, and the world who they truly were and

who they loved. And they were demanding to be treated equally.

On April 25, 1993, as many as one million people joined the March on Washington for Lesbian, Gay, and Bi Equal Rights and Liberation. They had come to the nation's capital to protest laws that discriminated against queer people. And they called on Bill Clinton, the newly elected president, to fulfill his promises to the queer community and to fight on their behalf.

When Drag Was a Crime

"Masquerade laws," which banned people from dressing in costumes, or in the clothing of the opposite sex, spread across the United States during the mid to late 1800s. Throughout the 1940s, '50s, and '60s, these laws were used by police to arrest many gay people.

There were also laws against people of the same sex dancing together.

Bars where gay people and drag queens gathered to dance were often raided by the police. When the Stonewall Inn—a bar in New York City's Greenwich Village neighborhood—was raided in the early-morning hours of June 28, 1969, the people inside fought back . . . and won. What followed was a nationwide movement for queer rights that continues to this day.

RuPaul took the stage in a red-white-and-blue Wonder Woman–inspired look. As "Supermodel" blasted from the speakers, a cloud of dust rose as thousands rushed toward the stage.

He couldn't believe where he was, gazing toward the Washington Monument, the National Mall stretched out before him.

There Ru was, standing in the same spot where Dr. Martin Luther King Jr. gave his famous "I Have a Dream" speech in 1963. RuPaul realized he now had a responsibility to the queer community. His days of running wild from club to club were over. Still, never one to take things too seriously, after the song ended, RuPaul told the crowd that he'd be back one day . . . to paint the White House pink!

After his performance, Ru received a terrible phone call. His mother had passed away. Toni had been ill for a while, and Ru had known this day was coming. Still, he was heartbroken. Toni had been one of his original inspirations, his first true fan, and the person who always believed in him. And now she was gone.

But RuPaul carried on.

The March on Washington, 1963

The civil rights movement of the 1950s and '60s saw African Americans fighting—through peaceful protest—for equal rights and protection under the law. Across the South, Jim Crow laws had separated the races—from hotels and restaurants to train cars and drinking fountains. And people had had enough.

Those who opposed equal rights for Black Americans often responded violently, injuring and sometimes killing the activists who were calling for change. With new laws stalled in the United States Congress, the March on Washington for Jobs and Freedom was organized by Dr. Martin Luther King Jr. and other leaders to demand that these laws be passed. The demonstration took place on August 28, 1963, on the National Mall in Washington, DC. More than 250,000 people attended.

In 1994, Ru met his future husband, Georges LeBar, at the Limelight nightclub in New York City. Georges was "dancing like a maniac" when RuPaul approached him and asked if he could put his arms around him. Georges is six feet eight inches tall, and Ru was not used to people being taller than he was! (And Georges said yes.)

"Throughout history there are . . . windows of opportunity," Ru once said. During the early 1990s, "there was an openness happening" in America. And RuPaul took full advantage.

Ru became the first drag queen to be named spokesperson for a major makeup line, MAC's VIVA GLAM. He published a book about his life called *Lettin It All Hang Out*. He hosted a morning radio talk show with Michelle Visage, an old Club Kid friend.

In 1994, Ru made his feature-film debut in Spike Lee's *Crooklyn*, followed by *The Brady Bunch Movie* and TV shows like *Sister, Sister*. In 1995, he appeared in *To Wong Foo, Thanks for Everything! Julie Newmar*. The movie featured

John Leguizamo, Patrick Swayze, and Wesley Snipes—male lead actors known for their roles in comedy, romance, and action movies—all playing drag queens. Drag culture had come to Hollywood!

Wesley Snipes, Patrick Swayze, and John Leguizamo in *To Wong Foo*

But not all the attention Ru received was positive. Tabloid newspapers published untrue stories about him. Their headlines poked fun at him. He became the butt of jokes on popular TV and radio shows. But RuPaul always took comfort in the advice Toni had given him when he was teased in school: "Unless they're paying your bills, pay them no mind."

From 1996 to 1998, RuPaul (along with his cohost Michelle Visage) hosted one hundred episodes of *The RuPaul Show* on the cable channel VH1. He was the first openly gay man—and certainly the first drag queen—to host a talk show. *The RuPaul Show* featured big-name guests like the Backstreet Boys and *NSYNC, as well as Ru's childhood idols Olivia Newton-John, Cher, and—of course—Diana Ross.

How much higher could RuPaul's star rise?

CHAPTER 7
"Start Your Engines!"

RuPaul moved to Los Angeles in 1998 and continued releasing music into the early 2000s. But while new songs like "Looking Good, Feeling Gorgeous" were played on dance radio stations and in nightclubs, nothing reached the same level of success as "Supermodel."

Ru took time away from the spotlight to recharge. Despite his glamorous public personality, RuPaul was really a quiet, shy person at heart. Ru went on hikes and hosted barbecues. He spent time with Georges, friends, and family.

Ru's longtime friends and collaborators at World of Wonder—Fenton Bailey and Randy Barbato—were wondering what would come next

for RuPaul. They had lots of ideas, but nothing seemed right. Fenton remembers Ru once telling him, "I'll do anything but a competition and elimination show."

But by 2008, Ru had changed his mind. In the fifteen years since "Supermodel," no other drag queen had risen to RuPaul's level of fame. It was time to bring drag culture back into the mainstream—out of big-city nightclubs and into people's living rooms.

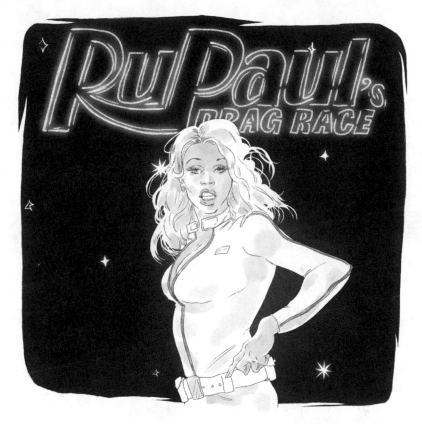

And so . . . *RuPaul's Drag Race* was born!

Drag racing is a race between two cars to see which driver crosses the finish line first. Courses are straight roads called "drag strips" and are usually about one quarter of a mile long. Naming the show "Drag Race" was a fun way to use a term people were familiar with for something that had never been seen on TV before.

According to Ru, *Drag Race* was a way to "celebrate the art of drag" and to "put a face and an emotion" behind it. RuPaul had already told the world his story. But there were thousands of other, lesser-known drag queens across the country who had their own voices and stories to tell. Ru wanted to give them the opportunity to inspire young people to be themselves and follow their dreams.

The first season of *RuPaul's Drag Race* premiered in February 2009 on Logo—a cable TV channel that aired mostly queer content. The show featured nine drag queens competing to win a prize package that included being named America's Next Drag Superstar.

RuPaul has described the show as a mix between *Project Runway* and *America's Next Top Model*, two popular competition shows for hopeful fashion designers and models. To win the title, America's Next Drag Superstar needed to show they had the most *charisma* (personality), *uniqueness* (originality), *nerve* (bravery), and *talent*.

Each episode starts with a "mini challenge"—a fashion photo shoot, for example—as well as

a "maxi challenge." On episode one, "Drag on a
Dime," RuPaul challenged the queens to create
looks out of materials from a discount "dollar
store."

Episode One: "Drag on a Dime"

As host, RuPaul plays double duty. He appears
dressed in men's clothes to lay out the rules of
the challenges, then later to check on the queens'

progress in the workroom. Ru asks the queens questions about their lives and what inspires them. And he gives them advice for how to perform well in the maxi challenge.

After the challenges, the queens must walk the runway on the Main Stage in their best drag. RuPaul hosts this portion of the show in drag. Having taken inspiration from actual supermodel Tyra Banks, the original host of *America's Next Top Model*, RuPaul plays every bit the tough critic, letting the contestants know exactly what she liked—or didn't like—about their looks and performances.

Next, RuPaul discusses with her panel of judges, which since 2011 has featured her longtime friend Michelle Visage. Ru listens to everyone's thoughts on who were the strongest and weakest queens of the week. But ultimately, the choice is RuPaul's.

After Ru names the winner of the episode, she announces the bottom two drag queens (those with the lowest scores). These queens must lip-synch to a song of Ru's choosing. Ru, the judges, and the other contestants are then treated to a dramatic drag performance.

Finally, Ru must decide whom to eliminate.

Borrowing lyrics from the song that made her famous, RuPaul tells the winner of the lip sync, "Shanté, you stay." And to the loser: "Sashay away."

RuPaul carries his message of love to *Drag Race*, too. At the end of every episode, RuPaul tells the contestants, "Now remember: If you can't love yourself, how . . . you gonna love somebody else? Can I get an 'Amen!' up in here?"

Amen.

Other challenges on *RuPaul's Drag Race* have included the queens writing rap verses to songs, learning dance numbers, performing stand-up comedy, filming TV commercials, and hosting their own talk shows—many of the things RuPaul himself had done over the years. Before they can even *think* about winning the crown, RuPaul's queens needed to *work*!

BeBe Zahara Benet, the first winner of *RuPaul's Drag Race*

Not many people tuned into *RuPaul's Drag Race* in 2009. But with each new season, the show gained more fans. In 2016, *Drag Race* won an Emmy award, the first of many more to come. For its ninth season, in 2017, *Drag Race* moved from Logo to VH1, and its viewership doubled. Now it is regularly the most popular cable show in its time slot. In 2019—across cable, streaming, and online—the show was watched more than 190 million times!

Bob the Drag Queen

Over thirteen seasons (and counting) and more than 170 episodes of the show so far, fans have met drag queens from all corners of the country and from many walks of life.

Hilarious queens like Bianca Del Rio and Bob the Drag Queen. High-fashion queens like Raja and Aquaria. Accomplished dancers like Alyssa Edwards and Shangela. Kooky queens like Jinkx Monsoon, and queens who sometimes dressed more like monsters than glamorous women, like Sharon Needles and Yvie Oddly.

Shangela

"[These queens] are teaching young people how to . . . find their light and to shine in that light," RuPaul said.

As the show's popularity skyrocketed, more famous celebrities appeared on the show as guest judges—stars like Lady Gaga, Miley Cyrus, Christina Aguilera, Nicki Minaj, Neil Patrick Harris, and Adam Rippon, to name a few.

And if you think RuPaul's star couldn't shine any brighter . . . hunty, she is just getting started.

Lady Gaga and RuPaul

Drag Slang

Over the years, many of the catchphrases used by the queens of *RuPaul's Drag Race* have made their way into mainstream culture. While these sayings did not begin with *Drag Race*, the show has helped popularize some of them beyond the queer community.

Hunty or *henny*—another way to call someone "honey"

Yas and *werk* (or *werq*)—different ways to say and spell "yes" and "work"

Sickening—when something is so good, it makes you sick!

Slay—to perform very well; to kill (slay) the competition

Reading—to insult another queen but in a clever and playful way

What's the T or *tea?*—the "T" stands for "truth";
to "spill tea" is to speak the truth

Kiki—to gossip, to spill tea

CHAPTER 8
"Werk" the World

RuPaul and his award-winning TV show have taken the world by storm.

Ru continues to record new music and regularly features his songs, like "Cover Girl" and "Sissy That Walk," on the *Drag Race* Main Stage. He has published new books—*Workin It!* (2010) and *GuRu* (2018)—and has appeared in TV shows like *The Simpsons* and *Ugly Betty*. He also stars in his own scripted Netflix series, *AJ and the Queen*.

RuPaul's Drag Race has also spawned spin-off shows, all of which RuPaul hosts and works on as an executive producer. On *Drag U*, women who feel like they've lost their sense of glamour and confidence are given "drag makeovers" and life lessons by drag-queen "professors." On

RuPaul's Secret Celebrity Drag Race, famous men—and women—are put into drag by queens from the show. There have also been multiple seasons of *RuPaul's Drag Race All Stars*, a series in which queens who performed well on their seasons return to compete for a spot in the *Drag Race* Hall of Fame.

The *Drag Race* phenomenon has also gone global, with international versions of the show airing in the United Kingdom, Thailand, Chile, and Canada. *Drag Race* queens have teamed up and toured the world together. In 2020, a number of fan-favorite queens—including Naomi Smalls and Asia O'Hara—starred in a live stage show that ran for more than a month at the Flamingo Las Vegas Hotel and Casino.

In 2015, the first RuPaul's DragCon, a convention for all things drag, drag queens, and *Drag Race*, took place in Los Angeles. It expanded in 2018 to New York City, and in 2020 to London, England. Thousands of fans go to these conventions every year.

At DragCon, fans can buy anything they need for a fabulous drag look, attend panel discussions, meet queens from the show, and watch drag performances. Some DragCon attendees come in drag themselves!

Many of the fans are teenagers or younger. "Parents come up to me . . . and say [the show] helped them understand their queer child a little bit more," Michelle Visage said. "This little TV show has changed and saved so many people's lives."

"That's the revolution right there," RuPaul said of these young fans. "They are our hope for the future."

In 2018, RuPaul was honored with a star on the Hollywood Walk of Fame. Jane Fonda, one of Ru's childhood idols, presented him with the honor. But she said the star "should be at least three sizes bigger" because no one "else has ever launched an industry like RuPaul has. . . . Behind the glamour," she said, ". . . is a man of great depth, incredible intelligence, and compassion."

People around the world have embraced RuPaul's message of self-love and respect. They have been inspired to express their creativity through the art of drag . . . and to pay their naysayers no mind.

"*Everybody* say love!"

Timeline of RuPaul's Life

1960 — RuPaul Andre Charles is born on November 17 in San Diego, California

1976 — Moves to Atlanta and enrolls at Northside School of Performing Arts

1978 — Attends first drag show

1982 — Makes his television debut on *The American Music Show*

1984 — Presents his showcase, *RuPaul Is Red Hot!*, at the Pyramid Club in New York City

1986 — Starrbooty character is born in Atlanta

1989 — Stars in the B-52's music video for "Love Shack"

1990 — Named "Queen of Manhattan"

1993 — "Supermodel (You Better Work)" music video debuts

1994 — Meets future husband, Georges LeBar

1995 — Releases autobiography *Lettin It All Hang Out*

1996 — Begins hosting daily talk show, *The RuPaul Show*, on VH1

2009 — *RuPaul's Drag Race* premieres on Logo

2015 — RuPaul's DragCon opens in Los Angeles

2016 — Wins his first Emmy Award

2017 — Marries longtime partner, Georges LeBar

2018 — Presented with a star on the Hollywood Walk of Fame

2020 — RuPaul's DragCon opens in London

Timeline of the World

1961 — Communist East Germany begins building the Berlin Wall to separate East and West Berlin

1969 — Uprising at the Stonewall Inn, a gay bar in New York City, inspires a nationwide movement for LGBTQ+ rights

1970 — First annual gay-pride marches held across the United States to honor the anniversary of Stonewall

1981 — MTV (Music Television) cable channel is launched

1982 — Madonna releases "Everybody," her first single and video

1984 — Michael Jordan plays his first NBA game

1989 — Berlin Wall begins to be torn down

1993 — President Bill Clinton signs Don't Ask, Don't Tell into law, which allowed queer people to serve in the military, if they kept their identities a secret

1997 — After more than 150 years under British rule, Hong Kong becomes part of China

2001 — The Netherlands becomes the first country in the world to legalize same-sex marriage

2010 — President Barack Obama repeals Don't Ask, Don't Tell

2015 — Same-sex marriage is legalized across the United States

2018 — In Sweden, Greta Thunberg begins a school strike to protest her government's response to climate change

2020 — NBA superstar Kobe Bryant dies in a helicopter crash

Bibliography

Braithwaite, Les Fabian. "2017: RuPaul Is Everything." *Out*,
25th anniversary issue, October 2017.

Lawson, Richard. "The Philosopher Queen." *Vanity Fair*, Holiday
2019/2020. Print.

"RuPaul Biography.com." **Biography.com**. Last modified April 16,
2019. https://www.biography.com/personality/rupaul.

RuPaul. *Lettin It All Hang Out: An Autobiography*. New York:
Hyperion, 1995.

Snetiker, Marc. "The Oral History of RuPaul." **Time Inc.**, 2020.
https://ew.com/tv/2017/06/15/rupaul-first-lady-of-drag-
lgbtq-issue/.